GROW UP FAST

LESSONS FROM AN AI STARTUP

ZACH RATTNER

Illustrated by
RITA SUS

To my wife Lindsay, who, as you will soon read, made the Yembo story possible.

CONTENTS

ABOUT THE AUTHOR

Zach Rattner, the Chief Technology Officer and co-founder at Yembo, is a software engineer with over 15 years of experience. He has a B.S. in Computer Engineering from Virginia Tech. Yembo is the leader in AI-powered virtual surveys with over 2 million videos inspected and customers worldwide.

Zach's previous projects include building a flashcard studying tool that scaled to over a million users and serving as the software lead for Qualcomm's internal innovation program, Qualcomm ImpaQt.

He is in the top 2% of contributors on Stack Overflow and has 18 granted US patents with several more pending. *Grow Up Fast* is his first book.

He has three children and lives in California with his wife Lindsay.

ABOUT THE ARTIST

Rita Sus is a professional visual artist of academic training with a background in art history and animation.

She is a big fan of aesthetics with a passion for detail and high-quality craft.

Through her work, she aims to create a space for contemplation where everyone is welcome.

—————

Rita's work is available at https://emit-light.com

INTRODUCTION

Nine hundred dollars.

To an early startup, $900 is a lot of money. However, we had just gotten our prototype working, and there was a big trade show coming up in our industry where we could exhibit. But the booths were $900.

Were we ready to spend the cash? We didn't have any customers yet. We didn't have any big venture capital companies behind us, or even any private investors. We had our own savings, and our spouses' patience (for the time being). Plus, we had a working prototype, at least most of the time it worked. What did it do, you might ask?

In the moving industry, a job typically starts with a visual survey. This is necessary because the moving company needs to understand how much the job will cost. Traditionally, the mover handles this process by offering to come to the client's house. He'll typically show up with a clipboard, pen, and paper. He'll walk around and identify everything he sees in the home, and write it down, as well as a rough estimate of each item's volume and weight.

In the living room, the mover might see two lamps and figure those take up about three cubic feet and weigh about 20 pounds. Over there is a sofa, a TV, a coffee table, and a loveseat. Add up the estimated weight, and a typical three-bedroom American home might be 8,000 pounds or so. It's more than most people think.

This is how the industry typically operates, and unsurprisingly, the sales process is not very fast. It's not unusual for a client to call in asking for a quote and still be waiting for an estimate two weeks later. The surveying process is quite labor intensive. It's also surprisingly expensive to do, because not just anybody can walk into a client's house and figure out how much a move will cost. The surveyor needs to be trained. They need to know what to look for.

You may not intuitively think this, but about 40 to 50% of a typical move's weight is composed of the packing materials alone, so the "art of the estimate" is not just seeing a bed and a lamp, it's also about seeing how many boxes are going to be needed to pack up that lamp, the kitchen, or the garage.

Add it all up and the sales process is fairly slow. If one were to be able to speed this process up, the mover would be able to make more money.

This is what our fledgling prototype accomplished, or at least we thought it would. No one had actually used it yet at this point, but the bones were there.

In 2017, we built a prototype application powered by custom artificial intelligence (AI) technology. It allowed someone to take a video with their phone; just 20 or 30 seconds per room was sufficient. They'd upload the video, and the AI would identify the items in the video. The mover could get a visual inventory list with the items, volumes, and weights detected automatically. It was a prototype, but it worked. Most of the time.

I say prototype because the technology wasn't quite reliable yet. For example, it would see a lamp and be 82% sure it was a lamp. To a mover, it's not exactly clear what to do if something is 82% sure to be a lamp. The AI sometimes confused televisions for microwave ovens, because both are rectangular. We had developed the technology sufficiently to get the idea across, and if you were an enterprising moving company you could actually use it to quote a job. We knew what we needed to work on next, and we were making progress every day.

We felt we were ready to approach potential customers.

At first, we started cold-calling different moving companies, trying to interest them enough to ask them to sign letters of intent to use our product, so that we might do a paid pilot next. Then we heard about this moving and storage industry trade show. But the booths were $900.

Thinking laterally, I figured I could go to the show, and hang out at the bar instead. I did the math in my head and figured that at $9 a beer, I could talk to 100 prospects at the bar for the same amount of money as buying a booth. If I bought a booth, it's possible no one would stop by. But at the bar, if you can muster the confidence, you meet people.

We did wind up talking to many people at the bar, and most of the reactions fell into one of two camps. The optimists told us, "Wow, if you make this work, it's going to revolutionize the industry." Others were skeptical. We were also told, "You're full of hot air" (sometimes something nastier).

We did find one moving company that turned out to be a serious lead. They understood what we were trying to do. We went through long negotiations over money and exclusivity, especially exclusivity, because they wanted to lock their competitors out of the product.

It was absolutely one of the most stressful times in my life. We had sold the idea to the internal tech team at the moving company but not to the actual movers who would be using the product each day. We had an end-to-end workflow implemented, but there were valid questions about whether we had reached the "viable" aspect of a minimal viable product.

We went ahead with the deployment, but rollout was slow. The usage was low, and when results came back, people were having a hard time making sense of the results. In retrospect, I see now we didn't have a direct line of contact to the actual users, so training wasn't really going that well. The people distributing our product understood it, but not the users.

We believed in the product and its potential. We had an acquisition offer on the table from the company that would have made my co-founder and me a lot of money, but it didn't feel right to take the money and run.

We knew we were on to something that could disrupt, in a positive way, the home services industry, and we really weren't into the business to make a quick buck.

We didn't have all the pieces of the puzzle. We had not built up sales, marketing, or product management functionality. It didn't feel like we were true founders of a company yet. It just felt like we had made a really cool demo.

We bit the bullet and turned down the acquisition offer, and the customer walked. We were back to square one. Actually, square two because the product had matured. But we realized we needed to work directly with the buyers in a more typical software-as-a-service way. With no exclusivity.

Fortunately, we had some breathing room because we weren't burning much cash, and we didn't have many employees.

So, what to do now?

A trade show.

A proper trade show this time, with a proper booth that showed off our technology.

This time we spent the $900 for the booth. Actually a bit more than that because we paid extra to be in the same aisle as the buffet lunch. If you've ever been to a trade show, you know that nobody misses the buffet lunch. But how did we make sure people stopped by the booth?

Naturally, we trained an AI algorithm to detect people. We set up a giant TV and pointed a camera at the end of the buffet line. When someone was picking up their silverware and napkins, our AI would detect them, draw a box around them, and show the probability the AI was confident it was looking at a human. When the people at the buffet looked up to find a place to sit, they would see this big TV screen in our booth with their picture on it and a box drawn around it which said "Human: 97%"

Of course, people stopped by because they wanted to say "That's not right. I'm 100% human!" Most were.

This allowed us to start a conversation about identifying furniture rather than humans. Just like you'd expect to happen in a book about startup businesses, we racked up a backlog of people wanting to use our product. So many, in fact, that we couldn't service them all at once!

The trade show saved us. We didn't die.

It took us about a year to put together a sales function, figure out our pricing, our success metrics, how we do training, our refund policy — in other words, all the kinds of things that make a viable business. The company became more mature, and I felt like a real founder because I had to deal with all aspects of the business, not just the technical and engineering parts.

I realized during this process that I couldn't just be an engineer building a cool prototype anymore. I had to master all the moving parts of a startup.

We were building a real business with a product that other real businesses would depend on.

I was building a business that my family and the families of the employees would depend on for their livelihood. If I did this, hundreds, perhaps thousands of people would depend on … me.

I realized that I had to grow up fast.

This book explains how I did.

Why Did I Write This Book?

Most business books are written by professionals later in their careers than I am. Why write a business book now, when I'm still in the thick of things? For me, there were two driving factors:

1. As my company has grown, I've found myself repeating certain lessons I've learned to teammates, mentees, and friends. I've seen folks achieve tremendous accomplishments in short amounts of time. This inspired me to consolidate the lessons so they can be shared more easily.
2. The pace of change that AI is bringing is too fast to sit on the sidelines. Industries are rapidly adjusting to realize the benefits and mitigate the

risks brought along by this nascent technology. I wanted to share the lessons now, since no one knows what the world will look like decades from now.

Who This Book Is For

This book is geared toward people looking to grow up fast in business in the era of AI:

- Students
- Early career tech professionals
- New or prospective startup founders
- New managers
- Experienced professionals who are new to AI

How to Use This Book

There are several ways you can use this book:

- You can read it like a novel.
- You can refer to the Table of Contents and skip to the sections that are most relevant for your situation.
- You can keep it on your shelf and refer to particular topics as they come up.

What This Book Is Not

There are many resources available on the topics of business and AI. This book does not attempt to be all-encompassing. It is not:

- A textbook on computer vision or machine learning. You do not need an advanced mathematics background to read this book.
- A guide on fundraising. While the lessons within touch on certain aspects of being venture-backed, this book is not intended to be a primer on raising venture capital.
- An infomercial for Yembo or myself. The stories covered within this book are drawn from my own experience, but it was my goal to extract the lesson learned from the experience as opposed to drawing excessive attention to myself.

A Brief Timeline

You may not know me or my startup Yembo already, so allow me to quickly fill you in:

- **2011**: I graduate Virginia Tech with a computer engineering undergraduate degree. My first full-time job after college is at the telecom giant Qualcomm working on software for cellular modems.
- **2015**: The most advanced algorithms become more accurate than humans at object identification tasks. I don't contribute to this particular achievement, but it opened up a plethora of possibilities.
- **2016**: I leave Qualcomm and do consulting projects to pay the bills while I figure out my next steps.

- **2017**: Yembo takes its first round of outside investment and the founding team is assembled.
- **2018**: Yembo launches its first product, a computer vision platform for moving companies to streamline their estimation processes.
- **2019**: Yembo's client base expands internationally to Europe and Oceania.
- **2020**: Yembo raises a venture round to add a new business unit serving the property insurance industry.
- **2022**: Yembo's products are processing hundreds of hours of video every single day.

I've learned the lessons in this book largely through trial and error and the high stakes of working at a startup in a nascent area of technology. The lessons are not complete by any means. Do bear in mind that I am still growing up just like everyone else. But I figured if something I've experienced can help someone else propel to new heights, it'd be better to share than to keep to myself.

PART I

GETTING STARTED

"This one's optimistic"

Optimistic • Radiohead • Kid A

1

THE FUTURE ON LINE ONE

Remember way back in the old days, when a madcap dream, a pinch of luck, and a cordless hair dryer could kickstart your startup career?

I do.

In the spring of 2015, I worked as an engineer at the telecom giant Qualcomm, nearly a $100 billion company that designs and markets wireless communication technology. Have you ever owned an iPhone? Chances are there is a Qualcomm chip inside.

I had a great job at a great company. Interesting work. Great people. I got to meet the engineer who invented airplane mode. Commute in, commute home. Company man. Life was good.

Why would I change anything?

As a student at Virginia Tech, I had ambitions to do a startup eventually, but I figured it'd be best to get some real-world experience under my belt before that. Hence, I was working at Qualcomm.

Some people are born entrepreneurs, but I'm not sure I

was. Research shows that 9% of future founders are committed to starting their own business by age nine and another 6% by age 13.[1] Notably, people considering starting a company before age 15 have a very high failure rate. There is a significant decrease in business failures if the individual first considers starting her own business after her 15th year. After the age of 21, the average failure rate declines rapidly.

This may be because if you choose to go into your own business after the age of 21, you can take into consideration other life experiences such as college, which may help you make more rational decisions.

In my senior year in college, I applied to several tech companies and landed at Qualcomm right when 4G technology took off. After a few years in, I was now a senior engineer, which was one level up from entry-level. There were probably 10,000 other engineers at the company with my same title. We all had great jobs at an exciting time in the industry.

———

The day that changed my life was like any ordinary workday. I spent many working days in a telecom lab filled with simulated cell tower base stations. Only getting two signal bars? I know why. I promise it's pretty fun.

We were working on software that phones would use to hand off the call from one cell tower to another without dropping. Even if your phone is moving down the highway at 80 miles per hour, the radio signal needs to transfer seamlessly from one tower to another (even though it probably shouldn't because you'd be speeding). If you are in an urban environment where radio signals reflect off skyscrapers like light bounces off a mirror, your phone still needs to transfer correctly and keep its signal.

It was a technically challenging and mentally stimulating job. I felt like I was solving puzzles all day. Around six or so in the afternoon on this particular day, I packed my bag and headed home.

On my commute home in the car, I received a call from a number I didn't recognize. Most of the time, I don't pick up a call from an unknown number because it could be an enthusiastic telemarketer trying to sell me a lifetime supply of something I don't need. It's my usual practice to let those mystery calls go to voicemail and savor the element of surprise later (or never).

I picked up the call for some reason, most likely traffic-induced boredom. I am sure glad I did — it was Steve Altman, former president and vice chairman of Qualcomm. Oh, boy.

Steve joined Qualcomm in 1989 as a lawyer and worked his way up through the strength of his work in designing and negotiating license agreements for Qualcomm technology.[2] His contributions were crucial for growing the company into a juggernaut.

Steve had recently retired from Qualcomm and was managing a portfolio of investments. We had met briefly earlier in the year for another project, and frankly, I was surprised he remembered my name, much less wanted to speak with me.

He asked if I had a minute, which I did because... traffic.

We exchanged pleasantries, and then he dropped a question I didn't see coming, a question that no one in their right mind could see coming.

"What do you think of a battery-powered hair dryer?"

I didn't.

Never have.

Why would I?

Why would Steve?

I have had the same short haircut since I was a teenager. But there I was, stuck in traffic, and one of the most influential people I had ever met was asking me for my opinion on the matter. Interesting.

I told him a battery-powered hair dryer seemed like an exciting idea, but whoever wanted to make such a thing would need to be careful about the weight and that if this feat were easy to pull off, I'm sure it would have been done by now. He mentioned he had a contact interested in building one and asked if I'd be willing to meet.

I had a lot of reservations and doubts, not the least of which was that I am a software engineer by training with virtually no experience in hardware design. Or manufacturing. Or consumer electronics. Or especially battery-powered hair dryers.

Steve didn't seem interested in grilling me on my limited qualifications for working on this idea, and I certainly wasn't about to initiate that line of inquiry. I did my best to set reasonably low expectations and agreed to meet the founders of VOLO Beauty, the startup pursuing this project in which he was considering investing.

We said goodbye. I stared ahead at the line of cars.

Battery-powered hair dryers?

In hindsight, no official degree or credential deems one ready for startup life. It's been my experience that many people feel the threshold to make that leap is just a little past their current abilities. Maybe they need just a bit more experience before they think they will be ready.

I was one of those people. I'd been thinking about a startup for years, and now Steve was calling my bluff. Uh oh.

And speaking of calling, nothing in the rest of this book would have happened if I had not taken that call.

Lesson Learned: When in doubt, pick up the phone.

2

PUTTING IN THE WORK

So I did it.

I ended up leaving Qualcomm and took on consulting gigs to buy time to figure out how to transition to a startup founder.

Not only was this a career change, but a mindset change.

Step one was becoming clear — building this hair dryer for VOLO Beauty. Step two was supporting myself in the meantime. To whit:

I worked on an app for personal trainers to help them manage their business. The app was not doing particularly well, and the person responsible for their IT infrastructure had flown the coop. I worked with them part-time to keep their systems running. It paid the bills, and the people were friendly.

I built a paperless billing solution for an asphalt trucking company, which is a more exciting business than it sounds. Why? Because asphalt is literally a perishable product (like bananas, only heavier, and harder to peel) that must be delivered promptly. If you think about it, modern society entirely depends on asphalt.

Almost every industry is fascinating if you dig into it. I didn't know anything about the book business before I wrote this book. The framework of the business is fascinating. The proofreading, not so much.

I set up an embedded system technology stack for a wireless Internet of Things startup, which was helpful because I got to observe many things about manufacturing that I'd never seen before. It's one thing to dream something up. It's quite another to build it. Which I was soon to learn.

Lesson Learned: Sometimes the businesses that appear the most boring are the most vital.

These jobs got me by while I got to work on the, um, hair dryer.

Since I happily knew so little about the hair dryer space, I could ask basic questions without fear of judgment. I didn't have the luxury of being able to come across as an expert, so I figured I should start by asking good questions.

So, as Mark Watney says in *The Martian*, "Work the problem."[1]

Sometimes our skills get the better of us — we gain mastery in an area, others respect our work, then we start building expectations that all we do needs to be at a certain level of quality. The fear of returning to square one can keep us from trying new things. Fortunately, I don't mind returning to square one, so that's where I went.

I read up on the history of hair dryers. In 1888, as new appliances entered the market, French inventor Alexandre Godefroy filed the first patent for a hairdressing device.[2]

Godefroy's persistence and innovation is a textbook entrepreneurial example of product iteration, whereby you accept that no product is perfect from the outset, but that the best way to create a great product is to refine and improve it continually.

By modern standards, his invention is hardly recognizable as a hair dryer. Or anything of human origin. It was intended to be connected to a heat source (fire) utilizing a pipe and featured an escape valve to regulate the heat (uh-huh) and avoid scorching the noggin of the hapless "dry-ee" or as we like to call them, "plaintiff." To give credit where credit is due, the invention was ambitious — it could perform all sorts of hair styling skullduggery such as shampooing, rinsing, and even shaping wigs (into tiny burning crisps).

A. E. GODEFROY.
HAIR DRESSING DEVICE.

No. 389,803. Patented Sept. 18, 1888.

Figure 1 from US Patent No. 389,803

I channeled my inner Godefroy and set to task:

1. The CEO sent me a bunch of hair dryers. That was a special day in my life.
2. I weighed them. That was input number one.
3. I measured the power they drew on various settings. More inputs.
4. I then took them apart to see what was inside.

Power is the critical factor in this type of device. After a weekend of tinkering, I learned enough about how hair dryer electronics worked to hold down an intelligent conversation on the schematics of hair dryers. This made me a much sought-after guest at dinner parties.

I also studied battery technology and its units of measure. By back-of-the-envelope math, I determined that if I were to go to a remote-control car hobbyist store and buy commercial, off-the-shelf battery packs, I'd need at least eight pounds of batteries to be able to power a traditional 1800-watt hair dryer.

Drying your hair with a device this heavy would be more like deadlifting than hair drying. Mike Tyson's boxing gloves weighed 18 ounces.[3] My hair dryer would weigh as much as nine of Mike Tyson's gloves. Not gonna happen.

I shared my findings with the founders, and we got to brainstorming. This is where breaking big problems into small ones is helpful and fun. We worked the problem:

1. Much of the power a hair dryer consumes goes to the heating element. Only about 10 to 20% goes to other components like the fan.
2. Most heating elements found in hair dryers are resistive wires, similar to what you'll find in a

toaster. Yes, basically, you're toasting your hair — food for thought.

3. Hair dryers must adhere to a universally accepted standard around safe operating temperatures. It's called Underwriters Laboratories (UL) 859. This taught me that the scalp should not exceed 114 °F while using a hair dryer, or the skin cells would start dying. It is one of the beauties of capitalism that entire conferences are held, and committees are formed to determine the appropriate temperature of a hair dryer.

4. Butane could do a bang-up job instead of a battery from an energy-density perspective. However, I didn't think civilization was ready for a butane-powered hair dryer. Yet.

5. There are two standard technologies used for motors — brushed and brushless. Brushed motors have, well... brushes to communicate to the motor when it should spin. Brushless motors replace this with fully electronic control. Most hair dryers use brushed motors, but most drones (another weight-conscious industry) use brushless ones.

6. There didn't seem to be any consensus among Amazon reviews on the ideal weight of a hair dryer. Some consumers were OK with heavier units; others weren't. Some of the units with the most complaints in the reviews about weight were about the lighter hair dryers, presumably because they felt cheap.

7. In terms of decibels, or the measure of the loudness of a sound, most hair dryers are pretty loud — between 75 to 90 decibels, which is about

as loud as the volume of an action movie in a
theater. This is because the dryer is held so close to
the ear while operating.

Traditional hair dryers advertise their wattage, but this
isn't a real goal from a consumer perspective. As audiophiles
will note, it is a similar principle to wattage on a stereo
amplifier, where more watts can actually be a negative.[4]
Wattage is not the actual result the customer cares about.

The late Clayton Christensen would ask, "What is the 'job
to be done' by the hair dryer?" Christensen, a Harvard
Business School professor, developed this line of thought (jobs-
to-be-done) to understand why customers "hire" products or
services to get a particular job done.[5] According to this theory,
people don't buy products or services per se, but instead, they
"hire" them to do a job.

The "job" a consumer "hires" a hair dryer for is to dry
their hair.

Most people don't care what wattage their hair dryer is.
They don't care about Alexandre Godefroy. They care that
their hair looks good and that it didn't take too long to get it
that way.

Thinking it through, the weight of the battery is directly
tied to how much energy needs to be stored, so if we could
reduce the power, we could use a lighter battery. That was the
best place to start since 90% of the required energy comes
from the heating element.

But how do you radically reduce the power needed in a
heating element that has existed for decades?

3

SPEAK THE LANGUAGE

Not knowing much (anything at all) about heating technology, we researched and found various categories of heaters. There are:

- Nichrome wires that are similar to what's found in toasters and traditional hair dryers,
- Infrared bulbs like those found in saunas,
- Ceramic heaters like those used in space heaters, and
- Some really scary ones that combusted materials. Awesome, but scary.

We brainstormed a few ideas for heating elements to try and worked on getting some prototype parts to test.

If it sounds like we were doing a lot of brainstorming during this time, we were. The best thing about brainstorming is that it's a creative act. When people think about creativity, they typically think about movies, music, or books. But solving engineering or business problems can be just as creative as writing a book. And creativity is almost always fun.

It's hard to call something "work" when it's something you enjoy.

Back to our story.

Initially, we took a conventional route and attempted to rely on external experts — source a vendor, get them under a Non-Disclosure Agreement (NDA), explain what we're doing, and ask for a quote. But this plan quickly ran into some problems. Most vendors didn't get back to us when we shared the NDA because they didn't want to be restricted by a company with no history or proven track record of shipping anything. The ones who accepted the NDA and learned what we were trying to do called us crazy and opted out after the first or second call.

Lesson Learned: Sometimes the apparent paths are not the most effective.

In much the way wattage turned out to be a vanity metric, when we learned that drying time was the actual metric, we decided to change course.

While sourcing vendors, we learned the language of each discipline. Thoracic surgery has its own "language." Plumbing has its language. So does the world of heating elements. So we learned the language.

Rather than explaining our use case entirely and being laughed off calls, we only told the heating element companies exactly what specifications we needed, which we could do, because we learned the language. However, few options were available for bespoke heating elements from local hardware stores. Once again, an obstacle was placed in my path. Where should I turn?

Alibaba.

If you want anything at all, the most random of parts or products, Alibaba, the massive e-commerce business in China, will probably have it.

In the market for some bulletproof glass for your golf cart? They have it. Lots of it.

Need 100,000 rechargeable lint removers? Not judging; it happens. No problem.

Just dying to buy a 30-foot outdoor LED billboard as a gift for that special someone? They'll ship that right out, and you'll be a hero on Valentine's Day. The day after, maybe not so much.

You get the picture.

So, I started messaging factories in Asia through Alibaba.

I found a factory that primarily sold infrared heating bulbs to convenience stores to keep food like nachos and hot dogs warm. You know those glass cases where the hot dogs hypnotically rotate under a lamp, and you can't look away? Yep, those. Why wouldn't those work? They should. They keep the hot dogs warm; that's their job-to-be-done, i.e., keep food warm all day.

Electrically, the specifications looked like they could work. Physically, however, the bulb needed to be about six inches long. Fitting this inside the head of a hair dryer would be challenging. Since a straight bulb wouldn't fit, I drew a horseshoe shape that I wanted the bulb to take, snapped a photo on my phone, and passed it along to the factory along with the voltage and wattage specifications I needed. The firm figured that I intended to keep nachos warm, and I didn't bother correcting them. I was speaking their language and it was working.

A few days later, a DHL package showed up at my door with the custom bulb. I plugged it into a prototype that I had soldered together by hand. Done and done.

Ultimately, the patent granted from this work and the actual product that we shipped retained the horseshoe shape:[1]

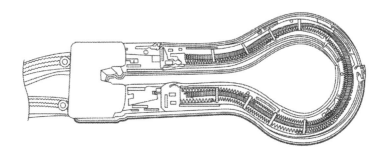

Figure 5 from US Patent No. 10,405,630

Next up was the fan. I figured drone manufacturers cared about minimizing weight in their propellers, so I stopped by a hobbyist store and got a drone motor to affix my fan to. A little hand soldering, duct tape, and hot glue, and the shape vaguely represented a hair dryer. Kind of.

The company's CEO I made this for owned a chain of beauty supply stores. I stopped by one and borrowed a mannequin that his stylists put wigs on and then used to train themselves on various hairstyles. I drove back home and took the mannequin inside. At night. Late at night.

Back in my secret hair dryer laboratory, which some call their bedroom, I took a spray bottle, dampened the wigs, and then timed how long it took to dry each with a conventional dryer.

Data, it's all about the data, whether you're measuring cell signals bouncing off skyscrapers or the drying time of moist wigs.

I then rinse-repeated the entire process with my duct-taped prototype dryer, affectionately code-named "The Knobster" for its giant knob on the power supply. Then I crunched the data. I stared at my lab book in disbelief.

The Knobster measured to within a few seconds on each wig. Whoa. This could work!

When you have an "A-ha!" moment like that, a breakthrough moment after a lot of hard work and worry, you should first celebrate, perhaps by firing up the 30-foot Alibaba LED billboard now sitting under a tarp in your backyard, and then immediately do one thing:

File a patent application.

Which we did.

Now, the next problem. I had to find an engineering team at a factory in China to try and transfer The Knobster to a feasible design for mass production.

Why China? Virtually all commercially-available hair dryers in the United States are manufactured in Asia. So, one month later, I was due to travel on a plane to China with the prototype.

At that time, the product was so new that I was under strict confidence not to tell anyone what I was working on. In a sense, our competition at that stage was time. What if someone else had the same idea and was developing it? We didn't think anyone was, but you can never be sure. But we assumed someone ultimately would because it was such a great idea. So, we were competing against time.

A friend who gave me a ride to the airport gave me unmitigated grief for not telling him why I suddenly needed to go to China. I mumbled something about "perishable asphalt." I later gave him a dryer after we shipped the finished product.

So finally, I was on my way, with a big bag of circuit boards and loose wires, which made for an entertaining encounter with the customs agent in China. I should have considered that potential hiccup, but how could I have? Everything was too surreal.

Just six months prior, if I had imagined myself in the following situation, I would have laughed out loud:

- I had a working prototype of a personal grooming product. We wanted the airflow to be configurable, so it had a large knob for fine-tuning. We had invented the great nickname "The Knobster" to boot.
- I was a named inventor on a pending US patent.
- I was collaborating with an overseas factory, talking about mass production.
- I was trying to explain to a customs agent in China why my bag held half the inventory of a RadioShack (if you remember those).

Honestly. How did this happen?

4

A FIVE-YEAR PROJECT

L ooking back at this long-term hair dryer project, I learned five critical lessons during what turned out to be my initial foray into the startup world.

The team behind the product needs to make sense.

The two founders of VOLO Beauty had complementary skill sets. The CEO, Ryan Goldman, had spent his entire career in the beauty industry and understood the complex web of suppliers, vendors, and relationships required to bring beauty products to market. His co-founder, Jonathan Friedman, held an MBA from a prestigious university, had experience with two prior startups, and used to own a machine shop — he knew the manufacturing process down to the most miniature mini lathe. It probably wouldn't have worked if either founder had tried to build such a company without the other.

The best products have some form of technical differentiation.

This may be my biased perspective as an engineer, but great products stand out. And to stand out, it shouldn't be trivial for a copycat to build a similar product. In my humble geeky opinion, technical differentiation is one of the best ways to stand out.

AirPods are a great example of this. Apple fabricated an entire chip line through their vast supply chain, the H series system-on-a-chip for the AirPods.[1] Because of this achievement, if anyone else tried to copy the complete feature set of the AirPods, it would be at least a $2,500 product, if I had to guess.

Validate as fast as you can by focusing on the riskiest aspects first.

All projects carry risks, but not all risks are created equal. By focusing on the existential dangers first, we could effectively zero in on a solution and then unlock other tasks. For example, the industrial design problem caused by incorporating the battery was significant, but the project would be nonviable if the heating element problem were left unsolved.

The overhead and cost of unnecessary side-mission projects can be avoided by tackling the riskiest projects first. This doesn't mean the deprioritized projects are unimportant; they are not *the most* important.

For example, the industrial design project was a significant effort and the product would have failed if it had been ignored. Still, by focusing on the heating element problem, the essential details that informed the industrial design were decided.

Learn to speak the language of your key collaborators.

Building the dryer requires knowledge of heating elements, battery packs, and airflow. The strategy of passing the problem along to vendors didn't work — if the solution were this obvious, other people would have done it already.

By breaking the cordless hair dryer problem down into parts and solving each independently, we were able to effectively work with our vendors, which required us to learn their specific languages:

The heating element company needed me to make a technology choice (nichrome wire, quartz tungsten, halogen, etc.), as well as my required wattage and voltage.

The fan company wanted to know the voltage, wattage, and rotations per minute.

The battery company required voltage, maximum current, and watt-hours.

Learning their "languages" enabled experimentation on each component and allowed us to rely on their expertise.

But in the end, it was up to us to bring all of these domains together and make the overall product work.

The buck stops at you, so make a plan that makes sense to you.

In a startup, you will encounter many stakeholders involved in some way with the company. Some will be more involved in certain areas than others: co-founders, employees, contractors, vendors, customers, investors, and competitors all contribute to and shape who the company becomes. However, as a founder, you have the most complete information.

It would be best to have a picture of how everything comes together and where things will be going.

So, while taking input from other voices is crucial, you cannot outsource your vision of where your company is headed. Decisions that are perfectly rational to someone with all the pieces in their head can appear crazy to an outsider with less information.

It pays to be mindful of this gap when taking advice from others.

On the surface, it seems ludicrous to talk to a vendor that predominantly supplies nacho snack cart vendors when you are trying to build a hair dryer. But I had the bigger picture and knew the electrical specs matched. It seemed ridiculous right up to the point where it worked.

Steve Jobs must have seemed ridiculous when he cannibalized the iPod, one of the top-grossing consumer electronic products ever shipped. His north star goal was to combine the iPod with a phone and then add an internet browser and other apps. With the picture in his head of what the iPhone would become, he knew moving on from the iPod was right.

My own north star goal was minimizing the time to dry a head of hair with the energy I could safely store on a device with a manageable weight.

And after five years of iteration, frustration, patience by my family, and a lot of fun with a great team, we had gotten there. Today, the VOLO Go cordless hair dryer is for sale on their website with many loyal customers. Need met.

5

MOVING ON

One of the most pivotal moments in my career came from my wife Lindsay not taking my advice.

We had been dating for a few years in college in Virginia, and I had a job offer to move to the west coast and join Qualcomm after graduating. After much discussion, we decided to play the long-distance game for a while. I accepted the job at Qualcomm and Lindsay surveyed her network to find a job that would let her save as much as she could as quickly as possible and move out to San Diego.

Lindsay got a job at a moving company, and things were going according to plan. But a problem quickly arose — Lindsay was quite good at her job. Too good.

She discovered that her company was preparing to invest significant resources into her development, but she had no plans to stay. They were sending her to training sessions for top performers and having her represent the company at industry events. She was torn. Even though she wasn't planning to move to California for six months, she didn't want the company to spend resources on her because she knew she would move.

I understood where she was coming from, but I reminded her that two weeks was the standard professional courtesy in business. Giving notice six months in advance would just put her job at risk. I encouraged her not to volunteer her plans and possibly hedge by not taking on the extracurriculars that would cause the company to invest heavily in her.

Fortunately, she didn't listen. She decided to tell her boss the plan six months in advance. After the initial surprise wore off, the company decided to find a way to allow her to work remotely. She was working in the international moving department, so there was even some benefit to her working from a different time zone. This time zone advantage would come into play for me later.

Fast forward one hectic year, and we were married and living in San Diego. Thanks to Lindsay's work-from-home agreement, our living room had morphed into the back office of a moving company. This was when I learned a fact that would inspire my first startup — why a visual inspection before a moving job is so essential.

Moving is an oddly compelling business. It's right up there with cordless hair dryers and perishable asphalt.

It is logistically complicated and labor-intensive. The industry generally operates on razor-thin profit margins; 3% to 5% is not unusual. Like Walmart, low margins necessitate high volume and accurate data.

An accurate estimate can be the key to profitability for a moving job. Typically, a moving company sends an estimator to review everything needed to move before the big day and then writes up a quote. It's not just a price that the estimator is looking to determine; he also needs to decide on the equipment necessary, raw materials, crew size, truck space, and many other details.

If you get one of these things wrong, the overall job can be a bust. For example, TVs are packed in special cartons to avoid breakage. Pianos have their hammers tied so they don't break in transit. There are dozens of details to look out for, and if you miss any of them, you can end up making quite a few mistakes:

1. Sending a truck too small and needing to make a second trip
2. Assigning too many crew members and unnecessarily increasing labor costs for the job
3. Mispacking something and breaking it

With our living room in the state that it was in, I got to see the implications of these visual inspections. I saw how smoothly things can go when everything is planned correctly and the horrors that can crop up if even seemingly minor details go wrong.

Wait a minute.

Visual inspections.

Vision.

As in… machine vision.

People who study entrepreneurs tend to refer to something called the "entrepreneurial event."[1] This mainstay of the field states that inertia often guides your professional behavior until something interrupts it. This might be negative, like a job loss, but it can also be positive, like winning the lottery. When it happens, this event gives you fresh eyes on a new set of opportunities that might be available to you.

The iPod was invented when an engineer at Apple realized

that the new Toshiba hard disk drives were tiny enough to fit in a small handheld device, which would be perfect for storing hundreds of songs in a compressed format and carrying them with you.

When an entrepreneurial event happens, the person has not changed, but in a way, their mental framework shifts. The potential to start a business was always there, but it needed a catalyst.

In my instance, the entrepreneurial event was my realization of the potential combination of AI and the process of moving. It's as close to an Archimedes-style eureka moment as I have ever had.

It was the catalyst that led to my first startup company, Yembo.

6

MACHINE VISION

Artificial intelligence.

Machine vision.

The most alluring technologies since the advent of the Internet.

Pull up your kombucha kegs, amigos; it's about to get nerdy. But I wouldn't put this in the book if this wasn't so important.

What happened with AI and machine vision in the last decade fundamentally changed our world. No, I'm not exaggerating.

Deep breath. Here we go.

You may have heard buzz around the term "machine learning" as of late. Machine learning refers broadly to algorithms where the behavior is learned from analyzing data rather than being explicitly coded into the system. Machine vision is the specific branch of machine learning focused on visual perception tasks. Think self-driving cars, autonomous drones, and algorithms of that nature.

In 2007, the AI researcher Fei-Fei Li began assembling a large dataset of images for use in benchmarking computer vision algorithms.[1] The language processing domain had an extensive lexical database called WordNet and listed their semantic relationships, e.g., "car" has a semantic relationship to "wheel."[2] There are WordNets available in over 200 languages today.[3]

The words were grouped into synsets, groups of words in a semantically-related language. I know, I know. Think of it this way — "The way my dog begs for food is so intense, I'm pretty sure he thinks 'sit' and 'beg' are synonyms in his little synset."

Back to Fei-Fei Li. The WordNet database is helpful in academic circles for developing and testing language processing and translation tasks.

Li's goal was to build something similar, but this time for images instead of words.

What resulted was the ImageNet Large Scale Visual Recognition Challenge, a 14-syllable competition that ran from 2010 to 2017.[4] Universities and corporate research labs would each submit their algorithms to see who had the most accurate object detector.

The inaugural test was a classification challenge, like a vast multiple-choice test, where the algorithm would be shown a photo, and the challenge was to decide what category out of the list of 1,000 best described the photo. There were variations on the challenge — requiring the correct category to match the AI's output was considered "top-1," and demanding the category to be present in the list of five most likely categories from the AI was considered "top-5." Naturally, top-5 error rates are lower than top-1.

Further complicating matters, the dataset included over 120 unique dog breeds. Accordingly, to master the test, particular classification skills were required. The dataset was first hand-labeled by human inspectors. Andrej Karpathy, a prominent researcher in the space, benchmarked himself and found his hand-labeling to have an error rate of 5.1%.[5]

So, an intelligent human will identify 19 out of 20 images correctly. That's our baseline.

In 2010, the best classification approaches used hand-engineered features, involving engineers building complex algorithms to define elements that comprise objects.[6]

For example, to build a chair detector, an approach might be to turn the image from color into grayscale (to make things a bit easier) and search for

- Vertical lines to identify the legs,
- A horizontal plane to make up the seat, and
- A vertical back coming up out of the seat.

This approach worked reasonably well, but detecting a new object was time-consuming — another example of competing against time.

For example, some chairs are office chairs with wheels on the bottom, whereas others are overstuffed. Some don't even have backs. A data engineer would have to account for all these variations. This approach is not easily scalable to a group vying to detect thousands of unique objects.

The main problems at the time were:

1. Reducing errors (beating what humans could do), and
2. Reducing the time such detections take to run

Then in 2012, something rather extraordinary happened. The AlexNet submission, designed by Ilya Sutskever (co-founder of OpenAI) and his Ph.D. advisor, Geoffrey Hinton, took an approach called deep learning.[7]

Their submission beat the runner-up by a whopping 10.8%.[8] The equivalent of ten years of plodding progress had exploded in an unusually creative solution.

So, what did they do? Rather than hand-engineering features, a deep learning approach consists of a network of layers that incrementally detect more complex features.

- An image is fed into the input layer and is handled by successive layers until it reaches the output.
- Basic features such as edges and contours are detected at the earlier layers. This might be the edge of a chin or an eyebrow in a face detector.
- Each layer builds on the last — it takes the previous layer's output as its input and feeds that data to its output.
- So while the earlier layers detect lines and contours in the face, the following layers detect mouths, noses, eyes, and ears, and the later layers assemble them and detect — ta-da! — a face.

The human brain biologically inspired this concept of a network of neurons. It is nowhere near a replica of the human brain. A high-end **NVIDIA** graphics processor such as GeForce **RTX** 3090 consumes about 350 watts of power, whereas the human brain runs on only 12 watts.[9]

But the real power that made this deep learning solution different is that it did not need to be hand-engineered.

Deep learning networks are trained by supervised

learning, which means that by labeling examples of images, the algorithm can learn what features make up what objects.

In the example of the face detector, a traditional approach would have involved hand-engineering the eye, nose, and mouth detectors, then assembling them together to make a face detector.

But in the deep learning approach, the algorithm learns independently from the examples it's already shown.

This means if you have a face detector but now want a pet detector, you update your training data, then the network learns on its own by following the examples. Each annotation on an image tells what is a cat or what is a dog, and importantly, each item that is not labeled is a counterexample — showing what is not a cat and not a dog.

Train on enough data for enough time, and the process can be refined, with the only limit being computing power.

After 2012, deep learning took over, and all the winning submissions used deep convolutional networks.[10]

In 2015, Microsoft Research won the competition with a deep network with over 100 layers.[11] The error rate had dropped from 6.66% in 2014 (Google) to 3.57%.[12] Remember, the human error rate was 5.1%. This means computers had finally become better than humans at recognizing objects in images, but... *almost nobody knew yet.*

Coverage of the tremendous advances in AI machine vision was relegated to mostly niche technology publications. It was baffling.

It was also an opportunity.

I wasn't an expert, but I followed the advancements in AI closely and understood the space enough to see that machine vision could be big in some instances. Really big.

That's when I knew I needed to do a startup. An AI startup.

7

THE VALUE OF DUAL EXPERTISE

S tarting out, I was not strong enough as an AI engineer to be notable in that space. And on the flip side, if I had only set out to build software that helps the moving and storage industry, I would have been one of many without a key differentiator.

But when you bring the two together, there wasn't anyone looking at the moving and storage space with an AI background. So, by becoming an expert in two fields (AI + moving), we were able to carve out a niche for ourselves and get a foot in the door.

To start a tech company nowadays, you almost always have to be an expert in the intersection of two fields. With the advent of the Internet and open-source software, the companies that could begin in a dorm room with minimal setup for the most part already exist.

While I'd love to be proven wrong with the hopes that new technology opens new opportunities that future wunderkinds can unlock the potential of from their dorm rooms, the more reliable path to success I have seen is to become an expert in two spaces.

When we were first talking to investors, we got a lot of pushback, e.g.:

- "AI tech is the future of self-driving cars, autonomous drones, and smart cameras. These all have the potential to be multi-trillion-dollar industries. So why moving and storage?"
- "Aren't you selling yourself short, Zach?"
- "You should go where the market is going, Zach."

It stung at the time, but in hindsight, I think the people who gave this feedback overlooked the value of dual expertise.

If you look at the overlap between AI and self-driving cars, it's a crowded space with many well-funded players. What I was most excited about was an area with untapped potential where people wouldn't see the advancement coming.

Moving wasn't the only market where Yembo's technology would be applicable — expertise building inventories for movers would pave the way to enter other markets as well. Movers don't generally move a few items in a home; they move everything. Yembo would have to identify virtually everything someone owned. The benefit of dual expertise clarified this pathway from moving to other home service industries.

Even today, many areas remain largely untapped by AI. Healthcare providers, restaurants, mechanics, and home improvement services are sitting on reams of data, and the potential is immense.

Lesson Learned: There are many untapped companies when looking at the intersection of a novel technology and an industry that hasn't been substantially influenced by that technology yet.

8

ARCS OF RELEVANCE

As a career choice, the startup route is not for everyone.

There are many easier ways to have a fulfilling career without taking the startup path, but at the end of the day, the opportunity at a startup is what you choose to make of it. The industry you choose to go in, the partners, customers, investors, employees, the entire ecosystem around the company is all something you can influence and, to a certain extent, control.

As regards Yembo, I had this nagging sense that AI for home services was ripe for innovation, and the timing was right.

It felt right in a counterintuitive way.

Take cutting-edge AI technology, but don't build a self-driving car or a drone or one of the few ideas Silicon Valley seemed obsessed with at the time.

Rather, apply it to a field that, in many cases, is still using pen and paper. That just might work.

I chose to bet on myself. The idea of fusing furniture and

relocation with AI appeared nearly farcical half a decade ago. Yet, now, it has nestled comfortably in the realm of the evident.

Betting on yourself is a difficult decision to make. The risks of miscalculating range from paralyzing fear to hubris. For this reason, it's helpful to consider the idea behind the startup.

When evaluating an idea, one way to gauge it is to look at the relevance of the idea given market trends and conditions.

Apple is one of the most recognized consumer brands, so its products are helpful for analysis. No product exists in isolation — they are conceived, designed, shipped, and improved upon in a particular time and culture.

In a successful scenario, the product's relevance grows over time and is iterated upon and improved; there inevitably comes a time when the relevance of the product wanes. This happens in most industries but is especially true with technology products, where the pace of progress is accelerated compared to other industries.

Some other underlying breakthrough comes along and renders the product obsolete, or customer sentiment changes, and the need isn't there anymore.

In 2001, Apple introduced the iPod to the world. Thanks to inexpensive and reliable storage, it came with the promise of 5,000 songs in your pocket. It wasn't the first MP3 player to market, but you didn't have to be a computer geek to understand how to use it. Sales started off a bit slower than you might think, but eventually, it took off and became a household name.

The success spurred variations, improvements, and offshoots. There was the iPod mini for runners and people who cared about miniaturization. Then the iPod Shuffle, for those who took the belief to an extreme. Technical advancements improved the product as well. In 2005, the iPod Photo came out and added a color screen.

Flash storage improved the reliability of the drives and replaced the spinning magnetic drives the earlier models had. These all contributed to making the product a category-definer.

Had Apple gotten complacent with the iPod revenue, eventually, the product would have faded in relevance and been replaced by something else. But under Steve Jobs' leadership, they phased the product out on their own terms.

In 2007 the iPhone was launched, and it was introduced as a mobile phone, Internet browser, and iPod all in one device. It did everything the iPod could do and more. The iPod lingered for quite some time, but Apple finally did discontinue it in 2022.

Before the relevance of the iPod waned, Apple came out with the next big thing.

By launching the next product off the back of the earlier one, they were able to enjoy the benefits of scale, distribution, supply chain, market attention, and make something bigger than the last one. As the iPod's relevance was fading in society, Apple's fortune had been effectively decoupled from it.

If you draw this out in a timeline, it looks like intersecting arcs of relevance rising, plateauing, and falling over time:

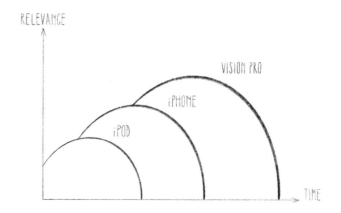

When deciding what bet to make — to do a startup or to stay the course, which features to include in the product, what industries to enter into, it can be helpful to consider the arcs of relevance for your business.

Pick a company you respect, and draw out the arcs of relevance for their products. They generally have a pattern of disrupting themselves before someone else does.

And if you have this mapped out for your startup and can't poke holes in the reasoning, well, then you may just be onto something.

PART II

GROWING PRODUCTS

"This one went to market"

Optimistic • Radiohead • Kid A

9

UNCOVERING A GOOD IDEA

After three years of working on the team at Qualcomm that managed signal bars, the company launched an internal innovation program. Employees could pitch ideas for new product concepts and compete for funding and resources to build working prototypes and help find a business unit to commercialize the technology.

The program attracted the kind of people I wanted to spend time with professionally. They were intelligent, ambitious, scrappy, and hell-bent on changing the world.

It was set up to take seven projects each year. Wanting to cover my bases and ensure I got in the year it launched, I went back through my notebook of ideas I kept by my bedside, pulled the best eight, and submitted all of them.

The strategy worked. Two ideas got accepted, and I had to pare it down to pick one. But more importantly, I spent a lot of time with the technical lead, Siddharth Mohan.

John had Paul. Steve had Woz. The Road Runner had Wile E. Coyote.

I had Sid.

My background was in software design and engineering, but Sid worked on the systems team. Sid's team worked on the underlying math behind the wireless protocols, and my team worked on the implementation.

Naturally, both our teams claimed credit for inventing the technology — his team made the standard, and my team implemented the software that made it real. You can decide who invented it.

After the program culminated in a pitch to the executive team where the projects were presented and then transitioned to internal business units, Sid's boss reached out to me with a job offer to serve as a software lead alongside Sid.

It was exciting but a bit scary too — I had a cushy job on a stable team. My manager then encouraged me to decline the offer, citing how most internal innovation programs at large companies only generally last a few years before budgets get reallocated.

I didn't know where I'd end up five years down the road, but I knew I wanted to spend time with people like Sid. I accepted the job and made the switch.

A few years later, my wife Lindsay and I were buying our first home. On a tour of a promising condo, our real estate agent was chatting with Lindsay, and it came up that she worked at a moving company. He also operated a local moving company, and they started talking shop.

What stood out to me was the similar challenges both moving companies faced. Here were two very different companies: Lindsay worked in the international division of a large company, and my real estate agent operated a smaller local enterprise with just a few crew members and trucks.

Both had real problems with inaccurate estimates. If both

companies had similar challenges with estimates, there had to be something here from a business perspective.

I texted Sid:

> Have an awesome startup idea. Use AI and CV to identify key items and automate logistics for moving companies.

Sid was out on a hike and didn't respond. The next day he replied to me about something else. The idea got lost in the noise.

I called him.

"Yes, I got your text."

OK, good.

"I thought it was the stupidest idea ever, so I didn't respond."

I always appreciated Sid's directness.

Side note — I didn't realize this then, but this is a maneuver in Sid's playbook — a cold-call to get a direct answer from someone. When negotiating with a counterparty such as a lease or a cloud subscription service, it's easy to delay via email or devise a heavily scripted response that masks genuine stances.

But if you cold-call someone, you can get a much more direct, unscripted answer that makes it easier to get a result, even if it's a no. I wish I could say I was using this brilliant strategy this time, but I just got lucky.

After some back and forth, I failed to convince him of the idea's merits, but I got him to agree to talk to my real estate agent and Lindsay's boss to learn more.

The more we learned about the visual inspection problem for moving companies, the more we realized that the problem wasn't limited to moving companies. All home service businesses run into similar issues requiring labor-intensive and time-consuming inspections as the starting point for an accurate estimate.

Moving was exciting in the home services space because people generally don't move just one room — they move everything. From a technological perspective, making just a good living room or bedroom detector is insufficient.

It would be best if you detected everything. And that opens doors from one home service to another. Moving was the perfect foot in the door.

That's what ultimately won Sid over.

Today we joke that he's the CEO of a company he didn't want to exist in the first place.

10

TEST YOUR ASSUMPTIONS

B uilding AI is an expensive and time-consuming effort. Before we started down that path, we wanted to ensure the problem we were trying to solve was even possible. Initially, we created a simple product with no AI — it just gave the mover the ability to send a link to the shipper, an interface to review the videos that came back, and a place to enter the inventory list.

We gave this early version to a few moving companies for free in exchange for feedback. Some of the most popular AI algorithms are biologically inspired. As a rule of thumb, if a perception task is impossible for a trained human to accomplish, it'll be challenging for AI to do better. We wanted to see if trained humans could perform the surveying job from videos collected through our software.

When we did this, we found that the time it took the mover to perform a survey decreased from 60-90 minutes to 30-45 minutes, depending on the size of the home.

And on top of that, the accuracy of the resulting estimate increased from a 60% error rate to under 10%. This indicated that the effort to build AI to solve this problem would be justified.

In essence, perception AI is just a highly efficient pattern matcher. Object detection networks are not using critical reasoning (yet); they are objectively assigning labels to items in datasets that have been painstakingly assembled. If these algorithms were capable of using critical reasoning, it wouldn't take so much manual effort to train them to do new tasks.

People tend to have a general misconception about AI, and I think movies are to blame. When you ask a layperson about AI, their mind generally jumps to humans being threatened by AI. *The Terminator* didn't help, nor did *2001: A Space Odyssey*, arguably the first exposure the general public had to AI.

In *2001*, the AI assistant HAL 9000 murders the spaceship crew he is supposed to be looking after. But those fictions paper over AI's genuine potential to improve the human experience in various unexpected and unforeseeable ways.

What Makes Deep Learning So Powerful?

In supervised learning, the branch of machine learning we were using to build our object detection algorithms, models are trained by providing hundreds or thousands of samples. The model is presented with images and descriptions of what's in them, and the AI learns what features are relevant. Once the model is trained, it can be used to detect items.

Because the networks are deep, the trainer doesn't know what precisely the algorithm will use to do its job. We intuitively know that a face consists of two eyes, a nose, and a mouth, but the algorithm is just given a set of sample images, and it learns what faces are on its own as it goes.

This principle is quite powerful in that the same code that detects pedestrians in a crosswalk could also be used to detect cancerous tumors in MRI imagery or prohibited items in an airport terminal. But there is a downside — the process of improving the AI — adding more categories of things it can detect and increasing accuracy on existing items, is iterative by nature.

For example, one of our earlier AI models could detect TVs in a house but not computer monitors. Our overall accuracy decreased when we came out with an update that added support for computer monitors. After investigating, we realized that because computer monitors and TVs are visually similar (black rectangles), we hadn't given enough context to the AI to discern between the two properly.

This kicked off the iterative exercise of providing better training data so the AI could learn more from context — computer monitors are generally on desks, where TVs are usually mounted on the wall or sitting on an entertainment center, for example.

The challenge with these kinds of problems is that you generally cannot know at the time when you are training the model where it will get confused. Your intuition can improve over time, but one of the tradeoffs you make when you allow the algorithm to learn independently is you no longer have direct control over how it draws distinctions.

We needed to collect realistic images based on how people's homes looked. It seemed obvious at the time to screen scrape Google Images or furniture catalogs — after all, didn't all this furniture people put in their homes come from furniture stores in the first place? But people's homes right before moving look nothing like beautifully staged catalog images, so the AI trained on this data didn't perform well. We learned quickly that we needed the AI to learn from actual scans of people's homes right before they moved.

Lesson Learned: When building a dataset to train AI, your training data ought to be as similar as possible to the real-world data you intend the product to be used in.

11

HONE YOUR VALUE PROPOSITION

Our first AI could only detect five distinct items. Look around the room you're sitting in. How many kinds of items are there? A chair, sofa, lamp, a desk? To have a viable business in the moving industry, five items are laughably inadequate.

We realized pretty quickly if we were going to have a viable business, we'd run out of time if we were chasing after an AI singularity. We needed to find a way to have an intellectually honest value proposition with AI that worked with the present limitations of our technology. Why would a moving company want to go through this process, let alone pay for the privilege, if we couldn't wholly automate things?

This is where spending time honing, testing, pitching, and refining the value proposition helped us sharpen our focus and define our strategy.

Defining Yembo's Value Proposition

A company's value proposition is a statement of the benefits a company provides to its customers. Some examples are:

- For a jewelry store: Exquisite gemstones with extraordinary craftsmanship
- For a grocery store: Fresh produce at affordable prices
- For a flight booking platform: The easiest way to find affordable flights

It can be tempting to jump straight to building once a founding team has an idea they are working on. I'd encourage taking some time to put together the company's value proposition, and test it by talking to potential clients. Refine it as you learn.

The idea we had in mind was that rather than relying on inaccurate phone quotes or slow and inefficient in-person visits, Yembo would allow the mover to send a link to a client, have them record a quick video of the rooms in their home, and identify what's there. There's no discrepancy if the move has an operational hiccup. Yembo would provide a timestamped video of what is moving with all the key insights extracted — the images of each item, the volume and weight estimates, the packing materials, and so on.

Lesson Learned: The value delivered to the customer is not the technology itself, but rather the benefit that the technology enables.

For us, AI wasn't the end goal. The customer values the ability to perform their surveys faster, at any time, more accurately, and with a visual record of what was inventoried. AI was just a means to achieve these benefits.

Setting the Strategy

With our value proposition defined, we did a study and found among a few thousand random home moves in America, over 98% of the unique items moved are comprised of only 200 different items. As you might intuit, items like sofas, coffee tables, and lamps are more common, and items like birdbaths, dog houses, and bronze statues are less common.

Our challenge was to improve an AI that can detect five items up to 200 without running out of resources.

To achieve this, we built an interface where the mover could review the AI results, make any corrections needed, and provide a visual report back to the customer. In one of the earlier iterations, the AI was so limited that it was only about 2% faster than the duration of an in-person visit. We had our work cut out for us. We spoke to over 100 moving companies and analyzed usage patterns in our product to confirm our value proposition.

At this point, the product wasn't suitable to everyone. Some prospects didn't want to experiment with unproven technology. Others were concerned about losing their jobs and didn't want to participate (thanks again, HAL!). Fortunately, there are thousands of moving companies in the US, so we could go down the list on Yelp and cold-call, email, or visit many local companies and refine the pitch until we landed on something that worked. Iteration again.

Even without a substantial amount of AI in our product,

our value proposition still rang true for the cohort of clients we were working with — we were saving the movers the drive time, which is a very real expense in terms of hourly pay, wear and tear on vehicles, scheduling overhead, and consumables like fuel. Plus, the asynchronous nature of reviewing videos allowed the moving companies to operate 24/7 without additional staff. Suppose a young working professional is out of their home from nine to five. In that case, the moving company can service them after hours by letting the AI analyze the videos when they upload after work and get back to them in the morning after reviewing the results.

In addition, we weren't just giving the mover a spreadsheet list of items; we were providing actual images of each item correlated back to the videos they came from. Rather than providing the mover with a tool to win an argument when an estimate later turns out to be inaccurate, we found we were preventing the debate from happening in the first place.

The transparency up front helped both parties to the transaction. The movers could write more accurate estimates because they could see the actual job at hand, and the customers were less likely to stretch the truth and ask for concessions because they had signed off on the visual inventory before the job was done.

Execution Time

Now we had a delivery channel for the AI. And the more it learned, the more value the mover received. On the path from incrementally detecting 5 to 10 to 50 to 100 to 250 unique items, the mover had a compelling reason to use the product that got better with each release. The time it took to review a job steadily decreased from 45 minutes to 30, to 15, and so on.

Looking back, the main thing we did right is we found an intellectually honest and compelling reason for someone to use the product when AI was in its infancy.

As with most software projects, almost anything is possible, but the question is how much time is needed to make the idea a reality. Our value proposition didn't change as the AI improved — it got better and more pronounced.

12

NAMING IS HARD

Brand names are incredibly important to get right, but in my experience, very difficult to invent.

Many people have asked what the name Yembo means and where it came from. An aspiring intern even approached me after an event and asked me if there was any relation to the town in Ethiopia of the same name.[1] The blank look on my face answered the question.

I wanted a brand name that met the following criteria:

1. Two syllables. Think Apple, Google, Facebook, Twitter, LinkedIn. The list goes on.
2. The .com domain should be available. I didn't want to be stuck with a .net or .co domain name.
3. Ability to be a verb, like Google or Kleenex.
4. Not offensive in any other language.

Naturally, this led me to writing a few lines of code that generated five-letter pronounceable names. Here's the code. If you follow along the notes you'll get it, especially if you like Scrabble:

```javascript
function generateName(pattern) {
    // Split the alphabet into vowels and consonants
    const v = 'aeiou';

    // Yes, "y" is a consonant. Get over it.
    const c = 'bcdfghjklmnpqrstvwxyz';

    // Start off with a blank name
    let name = '';

    // Continue through the pattern until all letters are used
    for (let i = 0; i < pattern.length; i++) {
        let char = '';
        switch (pattern[i]) {
            // Pick a random vowel
            case 'v':
                char = v[Math.floor(Math.random() * v.length)];
                break;

            // Pick a random consonant
            case 'c':
                char = c[Math.floor(Math.random() * c.length)];
                break;

            // Ignore anything else
            default:
                break;
        }

        // Capitalize the first letter
        if (i === 0) {
            char = char.toUpperCase();
        }

        name += char;
    }

    return name;
}

// Give it a whirl
generateName('cvccv')
```

Moving along, I ran the program and out popped some options:

- Cojbo
- Deywu
- Hivte
- Jogsu
- Jupvo
- Lavja
- Poxwi
- Pujzu
- Quqge
- Wagsu
- Wedxe
- Xulpa
- Yawto
- **Yembo**
- Yiwto
- Zigxu

Yembo.

Yem-Bo.

Yembo. OK.

Kind of rolls off the tongue. Not bad.

You can verb it. "We Yembo'd this house."

And with a .com available!

My co-founder initially didn't love the name, but neither of us could think of anything better at the time. There were no bad phonetic associations with it, it didn't rhyme with anything unpleasant, so it would do.

We ultimately decided to proceed with Yembo for the time being, and I agreed to be open to revisiting the name if he came up with a better one.

I'm still waiting.

I think founders at this stage tend to get hung up on

spending lots of time picking a name, when they could be doing actual work building the business.

To my point, Facebook. Or as the cool kids called it back at Harvard, The Facebook. Let's face it, Facebook is a horrible, awful name. Just rubbish. Face-Book. Sounds like an ointment of some sort.

I feel pretty confident they didn't bother spending months picking that name. More like, minutes. If that.

On the best comedy show of all time, the British TV series *The IT Crowd*, the cast mocked Facebook mercilessly and referred to it as "FriendFace."[2]

So, clearly, the name Facebook got picked quickly, and Zuckerberg started writing the code, getting the work done, and building the business rather than staring into his navel, ruminating about the absolute perfect name. He went with Facebook.

Until he didn't and changed Facebook to Meta Platforms in 2022 after paying a bank in North Dakota $60 million for the rights to the name "Meta."[3] You just know he and a team of shiny consultants with clipboards focus-grouped that name to death. He wanted it to reflect his move into the Metaverse, which, thus far, exactly nobody seems to be interested in.

And everyone still calls it Facebook.

Pick the name, move on, and get back to building.

13

DECISION TIME

It has been my experience that ending things is hard.

Thinking back to significant moments in life, the beginnings are usually scary and uncertain, and the endings are generally sad. For example, while we all intuitively know that the college years are temporal, there's still a sense of sadness as graduation ticks closer — friends will soon disperse. It's unclear which relationships will survive the test of time after leaving the college bubble.

I ran into a comparable situation at the start of Yembo. My wife and I had a long and thorough discussion about the project's parameters. From a spouse's perspective, the early days of a startup are quite like an expensive hobby — it takes a lot of money and time, much of it outside regular work hours.

And the payback period is uncertain and indefinite.

Naturally, she was concerned about this becoming an endless black hole of time and resources. And while I didn't see it that way at the time, looking back, putting boundaries in place early helped me focus and gave me an easy litmus test I could use to check myself along the way and see if I was on track.

Conventional wisdom says founders should take extreme measures like slashing all expenses to live an austere life to invest every resource under their control in the startup. While I agreed that dedication is essential, I couldn't reconcile that with believing we were sitting on the cusp of something big. And if we were really on the verge of something big, shouldn't I be able to find a way to make the finances work?

It's easy to emulate stereotypical images of success and give yourself the false sense that you're on the right track. But the best entrepreneurs I have met don't glorify the days of eating ramen and working until the early morning hours. You do it if you have to (and you will have to), but it's something to be minimized instead of glorified.

We ended our discussion with some firm parameters. I had a cap on our savings to put into the business. Beyond that, if I felt I needed more money, I would have to make it up by taking on consulting gigs.

In terms of timeframe, we gave it one year to reach the point where we should have revenue coming in the door. We figured if it took more than a year to get a paying customer, the business idea wasn't viable for the industry we were going after and the state of the technology.

Lesson Learned: There are no universally good or bad ideas when it comes to startup concepts. What is good depends on the founding team.

As a first-time founder with limited capital, I needed a

relatively quick path to revenue. For an established billionaire like Elon Musk, chasing Mars and brain implants are within reach. To each their own.

We ended up making it, but it was close.

It was around 10 months in when the first paying customer came through the door, but as we started to get our first few deployments, the demands on my time grew.

We had a working demo, but to make it valuable for users would require a lot of listening to customer feedback, building, shipping, and repeating. This process is impossible to pull off when you're also mentally elsewhere working on other people's projects for half the day.

To add to the stress, many of our deployments were offered at a low price point for an interim period to iron out the kinks, so there wasn't significant cash flow coming in the door.

I felt I was finding my rhythm with the consulting projects — I had a base of a few clients with whom I had a good working relationship, and things were going well. I had negotiated monthly retainers, so the cash flow was predictable. But I was finding the limiting factor was time — by keeping these engagements open, the number of people who could interrupt my day and control what I did in the day was too great.

I couldn't honestly sit down and work to improve the product at Yembo if a client could call me and ask for something, that would send my day sideways. Many words have been written about trying to serve two masters, and I felt the pinch.

Without a clear way out, I called a long-time mentor of mine to ask for advice. At the end of the call, she asked me,

"Do you just want to work for yourself, or do you want to make a product that can change the world?"

Immediately I knew what I needed to do. The consulting gigs needed to be wound down.

What came next was about 18 months of trial and error, and I used every spare moment I had to improve the product. I had some big problems to address.

Our initial version of the product showed the mover the AI analysis one image at a time, not for any great reason apart from the fact that splitting videos down into a series of images made the engineering easier to work with and the best object detection algorithms at the time operated on images. But it was cumbersome for movers to use.

Imagine looking through a living room you've never been in before, but instead of seeing a video of the room, you are seeing a series of six or so images, one at a time, and you're trying to double-check whether each item detected was seen previously in the room.

As it turns out, optimizing to make the engineering easy for us rarely serves the purpose of making something easy for customers to use.

The customers pay the bills.

The engineers *are* the bills.

Bob Dylan said, "You gotta serve somebody."[1]

Serve the customers.

14

EXERCISE: THE GRIPE DOC

W e learned a few checks and balances from our iteration process, which culminated in an exercise we call the Gripe Doc. Before we get into it, let's go over some workflows we have put in place:

Talk to your customers.

I've found in-person to be best since you can pick up on subtle cues such as body language, posture, eye rolls or phone checks that are easy to miss on video calls or written feedback forms. That said, video calls and feedback forms are certainly better than nothing — the important part is to integrate client feedback into your workflow.

Define a north star metric and have your iteration efforts seek to improve it.

This should be something concrete and quantifiable. It's ok to have a few but try not to have more than three to five, since too many metrics makes it hard to focus on any one. For us, we tracked the completion rate for the customer getting moving services and the time to review the AI results for the mover. Any feature we worked on needed to serve one of these goals, or we deprioritized it.

The top 10 gripes about your product should be changing each month.

Customers will always have feedback on things to change and improve. To track this feedback, you could implement a ranking system, even if it's something as simple as tally marks each time a customer asks for something. Even if you focus on the right things, you should not expect the list to go down to zero.

What you can expect, however, is for the particular issues in the top 10 to drop out and for the ones that replace them to become less consequential.

This is a strong indicator you are on the right track.

One sign we were onto something was that "the video failed to upload" dropped out of the top 10 and got replaced with "The product only supports small cartons being 1.5 cu. ft., but in Canada, they are 2 cu. ft."

Both are valuable feedback points, but the former threatens the company's viability if left unchecked, whereas the latter merely inhibits expansion.

Be as dispassionate as you can when getting feedback.

Don't take things personally — great engineers may be great at building, but the challenge at this stage is not the art of building but rather the art of finding out what to build. It's an entirely different skill set.

Meet the Gripe Doc

We use this concept of the Gripe Doc to test upcoming features. We find a small cohort of customers who are typically generous with their time and offer to give them early access to a new feature in exchange for feedback.

There is enormous pressure in situations such as these to seek laudatory feedback, but it's not entirely practical to cherry-pick the good and ignore the bad. That's where the Gripe Doc comes in. After someone tries out a new feature, we send over a Google Doc titled "<Feature Name> sucks because…" and we have them fill in all the things that sucked about it.

The Gripe Doc approach accomplishes two things. First, it reinforces the concept of relentless honesty. If someone is doing you a favor and you are generally polite with them, there is a societal pressure to sugarcoat feedback.

By telling them beforehand the product sucks and merely asking them to fill in the blanks, you are overcoming the ingrained psychological hurdle to be friendly and soft pedal feedback. As a result, you are much more likely to get helpful feedback.

Second, by setting this expectation up front and doing it consistently, the engineers took things less personally and weren't shocked to hear negative feedback about their features. Since we were shipping every week, there'd be an opportunity to have another conversation about the product in a few days. Hopefully, the work accomplished over those days moved closer to achieving the goal.

Contrast that with a hypothetical company of extreme

perfectionists who don't want to ship anything less than the best, and, as a result, only ship once every six months. Now each critique on the product is judging a significant investment of time and energy, and the team is much more likely to take things personally.

It's hard to get overly attached to any one feature if you only had a few days to work on it before exposing it to the harsh light of critical feedback.

Somewhat counterintuitively, I have noticed that the engineers who were the best students in school often struggle the most with receiving feedback productively. The same personality traits that make someone an "A" student often focus on relentless perfectionism, which comes at the expense of time.

Studying at a prestigious school is not a quick procedure. You study one thing for four years. Compare that with an eager engineer from a coding bootcamp who doesn't have the expectations of getting "A" scores on every assessment. Who will be more conditioned to try things out and take a risk?

When I first started, I expected the "A" student from a prestigious engineering school to outperform the bootcamp grad. However, in this stage, my experience has taught me the opposite — the bootcamp graduate has been much more comfortable making mistakes and iterating their way to the correct answer. The key difference is not about talent or abilities but rather ego.

There came a day pretty early on at Yembo when we had to hire a Customer Success team because we wanted to have more client conversations than I could handle, and I felt I couldn't do a very good job being dispassionate anymore.

When you only have one or two customers, you can talk often, and it's fine. I found it difficult to remain open-minded when I was working on a demanding roadmap and only had 30 or 60 minutes a week to take client calls.

One of my main regrets is that I never really solved this problem — I just swapped myself out for someone more equipped than me.

Here are some signs that things are going well in the early stages:

- You have a cohort of clients willing to talk to you at least weekly, ideally more often.
- These clients can be brutally honest about what is working and what is not.
- Your team is shipping fast enough that the top 10 gripes about your product are changing each month materially.
- The feedback your team is working on is generally weighted more toward addressing negative things than trying to make good things better. This may be counterintuitive, but we've found that when a feature is essential to someone, they tend to complain more about its limitations than brainstorm other things it could do.

Lesson Learned: By assuming the first version of your product sucks and making it easy for people to gripe about it, you can build a great product.

PART III

GROWING PAINS

"Pragmatism not idealism"

Fitter Happier • Radiohead • OK Computer

15

LOST AT SEA

"Come on, seriously?!" I muttered, my hand slamming down on the desk in frustration. My co-founder glanced over his shoulder at me and slipped on his headphones so he could continue his work in peace. I had been at this for a few weeks and hadn't shown much progress yet.

`CrashLoopBackOff` showed up on the screen one time too many for my sanity. We had successfully deployed our first working version of the product a couple of months earlier, and I was tasked with setting up the infrastructure so it'd be reliable for multiple customers.

If I'm being honest, infrastructure was a part of the overall product development process I had overlooked in the planning phase. There was so much buzz about building the product that I hadn't thought about the servers the code would need to run on.

Thanks to tech giants like Google, Facebook, and Twitter, customers have come to expect web products to be available 24/7 even if there's a power outage in the area, if a server dies, or if a million other people are also connecting simultaneously.

Yembo had a compelling demo that worked — you could click a link on your phone, scan a video in the web app, the AI would generate an itemized inventory list automatically and email the mover when the results were ready.

But some parts of the processing pipeline ran off my co-founder's workstation. If five people uploaded a video simultaneously, it'd be enough to bog the whole system down. Forget a million.

We had a problem.

To remedy this, I researched and decided to use a newer tool called Kubernetes to manage the infrastructure.

In marketing materials and tech news, Kubernetes was a buzzy technology with an almost mythical aura. Google had been powering significant portions of its search infrastructure off of it; then they open-sourced it, ostensibly as an onramp for purchasing Google Cloud services.

The industry was clamoring over how Kubernetes was the future of infrastructure because it allowed you to let code manage spinning servers up and down, automatically handling load and hardware failures.

Traditionally to maintain stable infrastructure, IT teams were built up to have people monitor servers. If a hard drive failed or the power supply died, the on-call engineer would handle sending traffic to other servers temporarily.

Whether you suffered from downtime or not was a function of how much excess capacity you had provisioned and how quickly your team could work under pressure.

This concerned me because it meant we would have to allocate resources not for product development but just to keep the lights on. If we couldn't hire someone, I'd have to handle it myself. I had worked in technology enough to understand the implications of handling it myself — servers seem to have an innate diabolical tendency to work perfectly during normal business hours only to die between 2 and 4 a.m.

On top of this, we were based out of San Diego, so clients in central or eastern parts of the country would start their day several hours earlier than we did. So if a problem cropped up at 4 a.m. for me, clients on the east coast likely would have encountered the issue while I was still asleep. Waking up to an inbox filled with disgruntled clients is not a recipe for success.

This is why getting Kubernetes to work was so important.

If I could get it to work and the tech blogs were to be believed, the infrastructure would practically run itself. In this scenario, I would be freed up to focus on improving the product, and I wouldn't have to hire on-call IT operations staff. On the other hand, if I were to fail in this regard, the product either wouldn't be able to scale, or we would have to divert resources away from product development to get it to scale.

What's a cash-strapped enterprising young company to do?

Swing for the fences.

We had to get Kubernetes to work.

And we had a deadline.

What do you call a challenge without a deadline?

Binge-watching Netflix, I guess.

16

BENT PRACTICES

On top of all this, it was early July, and my wife and I were due to have our first child in the first week of August. What happens if August rolls around and I don't have anything figured out?

I didn't even want to think about it.

The problem with Kubernetes was this was 2018, and expertise in the space was rare because the technology was so new.

I posted a job on Upwork, a popular platform that connects clients with freelancers. A posting for a typical web development or design task would get 200 or so applicants within 24 hours. But in this case, three days later, no one had applied. Searching for Kubernetes yielded just four matching profiles. I messaged them all. Two of them never got back to me, and the other two told me they were too busy to take on new projects.

Hence a long, slow, frustrating slog of me trying to figure out how to simultaneously learn Kubernetes and get our infrastructure to use it.

Our infrastructure was hosted on Amazon Web Services, so I wanted to run Kubernetes on AWS. I figured the risk of trying to learn another cloud provider like Google Cloud plus a complicated technology like Kubernetes was too much for the timeframe.

Thankfully I had a few connections at Amazon, and after persistent asking around (i.e., badgering), I got an invitation to their Kubernetes product while it was still in beta.

Responsible IT professionals will see this as a red flag — when reliability is paramount, it's not a good idea to use beta software. But remember the situation — I needed to figure this out in four weeks or who knows what comes crashing down.

Our infrastructure was a bit more complicated than most standard web apps — we had queues, AI servers with high-performance graphics processors, and we moved a lot of bytes around to process videos.

Just learning and spinning up a simple web server would have been a more reasonable expectation, but if I wanted to get all of our infrastructure off of Sid's workstation, I would have to figure out the AI servers too.

I wish I could say there was a silver bullet that made it all come together. There wasn't. We ultimately got everything working but through a lot of smaller initiatives.

I eventually found a contractor with some related experience but didn't have a lot of bandwidth to get things over the finish line. They acted more as an advisor who I could bounce ideas off of, but if I asked them to write code they would take too long to get back.

I tapped my network and coordinated a couple of troubleshooting calls with an engineer from Google who knew

Kubernetes, AWS, and NVIDIA to handle the graphics drivers.

I took notes as I went in case anyone needed to follow in my footsteps while I was on paternity leave. The guide to set things up was so complicated it surpassed 40 pages by the time I finished.

With about a week to spare before the baby came, I spun up the servers and finally saw `Running` in front of me instead of `CrashLoopBackOff`.

I don't think I've ever cried tears of joy at a terminal prompt, but this brought me pretty close.

Then to test things, I uploaded a thousand videos at once, logged into AWS and abruptly terminated one of the AI servers. Here we go…

Kubernetes realized, spun up a new server in its place, and redelivered the command to process the video that had been aborted partway through processing. The system was resilient.

Fast forward to 2023 and we still have not hired dedicated on-call IT staff. Maintenance is a shared responsibility of the engineering team, and since the team is distributed anyway, any time of the day is generally normal business hours in one of the time zones where we have the personnel. As a result, no one has to field 2 a.m. alert emails. Our system is reliable enough that we set up a way for the public to check our system's uptime at yembostatus.com.

We are consistently processing millions of network requests every day worldwide. Kubernetes had proven itself.

Sometimes technology lives up to the hype people throw behind it. That is a beautiful thing when it happens.

If I went into the Kubernetes setup project with an ego to prove, I might have been tempted to eschew help from others and do it all on my own in a form of nerd tech flexing. But given the time crunch, I decided to spread out the risk across multiple parties.

I took responsibility for the overall system coming together at the end of the day, but I wouldn't just bet on myself being able to figure it out, or AWS support to get back to me promptly, or my friend at Google who graciously gave me some advice after hours on a random workday.

Entrepreneurs are viewed as big risk-takers but are actually very good at minimizing risk. To whit:

Don't be paralyzed by the possibility of making a mistake.

I knew I had limited time and had to pick a direction. Plan A needed to work since I didn't have the time to thoroughly vet multiple options. This was inherently risky, so once I took that step, I did what I could to de-risk each step.

When I'd run into a problem, before spending hours trying to fix it, I'd write up a description and open an AWS support ticket on the matter in parallel. This way, I'd have multiple potential paths to the overall project's success.

Make decisions easily reversible whenever you can.

Decisions can't always be reversed — a strategic error made at an inopportune time can tank the company. But not all decisions are irreversible, and many don't need to be.

Sometimes bet-the-farm type scenarios cannot be avoided. Such is startup life. That said, even in such situations, it is responsible to look for ways to de-risk steps along the way.

Taking yourself out of the process can increase its reliability.

Entrepreneurs are generally good at starting initiatives. Great entrepreneurs are also good at handing off initiatives to focus on the next challenge.

Lesson Learned: Best practices can be bent when the situation is dire.

17

THE TIME WARP

C onstraints can be an awesome thing.
 They force focus and allow for creativity and
 clever solutions. Imagine solving a puzzle where it's
not clear what shape the pieces are or how many there are.
That's what solving a problem without constraints is like.

The problem is, constraints often come with societal
baggage that make them seem like a disadvantage. This is a
mirage. A fledgling engineering team at a startup might
lament, "We don't have the resources that a larger company
has," and they are right, but it's important not to overlook the
opportunity provided by constraints.

Apple ships free music recording software called
GarageBand that can handle 255 tracks of audio.[1] There are
essentially no constraints on what you can do sonically.

The Beatles recorded most of their albums on a 4-track
recorder.[2] It's hard to argue the constraints placed on their
recording technology hurt them.

At Yembo we have three main engineering hubs.

We are a remote company but have found grouping teams

roughly by time zone and with a common language is easier to manage than a dispersal all over the world.

Our main three hubs are in the USA, India, and Ukraine. We initially set the remote teams up due to cost, but as we grew we found it gave us a superpower. When we take on a new project, the system architecture and high-level design is generally done in the USA, most of the implementation is done out of Ukraine, and the QA is done out of India.

Thanks to the wonders of time zones, this works out in a way where during the work week we can make 24-hour progress each day.

A feature can be scoped out in the USA and the key components put in place, then when the USA workday ends, the Ukraine team implements more details, and the QA team tests it. Then when the USA worker comes back to work the next morning, they can review what was done and manage the next steps.

If you look at where 9 a.m. to 5 p.m. lies in each of these regions, you can see the effect:

One might think, after setting up this process and trying to learn to manage it all, I might find myself quite busy.

One would be correct in this assumption.

Amid our efforts, a trade show came around at which we were scheduled to exhibit. I needed to find an artist to help me put some presentation materials together.

The only lull I had in my schedule was around 7 to 10 p.m. in San Diego, so I pulled out a world map and looked for a landmass with working hours during that time.

I settled on Australia since there wouldn't be a language barrier and started hunting on job boards down under. I found a candidate who had a subtle reference to a Radiohead song in her Behance portfolio.

I immediately stopped browsing and sent her an email. She said she was available to work, so we got on a call and went over the project details. One project led to another and ultimately Yembo had its first designer.

It was our first and only candidate to be hired gradually over the course of several months. But we squared things away and over three years later, Rita designed the cover of this book. And drew the figures.

Over the years, we have found this time-zone-centric approach to be preferable to the traditional approach of a centralized team:

- Despite having 24-hour progress, the structure is sustainable over the long term because the individual workers are not burning themselves out — each group only works a typical eight-hour workday.
- The structure encourages the main engineer architecting the system to think through all the

critical details to be able to explain it clearly in prose in a ticketing system, which naturally discourages ugly hacks that often tempt time-strapped startups.

- Code quality is improved since there are multiple people involved, each of them tasked with slightly different jobs. Before a feature goes live it's not unusual for over 10 people to have interacted with it in some way.

Did we know all these things when we started off? Not at all. The benefits emerged out of a byproduct of a constraint.

18

EXERCISE: THE TIMESHEET ANALYSIS

T ime.

One of the most commonly constrained resources at a startup is time.

There are so many things to do and not enough time to do them all. Sometimes cliches are true for a reason.

On top of that, the problems that are the most obvious are not always the most important. Instant messaging tools like Slack do not help with this. The cost in terms of time and mental energy to send a message is asynchronous with respect to the time it takes to respond.

Consequently, as a founder, it is easy for your day to be completely consumed by a lot of small questions from others that collectively add up and knock out the bulk of your working hours. This can also be exacerbated by a host of other reasons, such as client calls, product feedback discussions, back office support work, and on-call alerts when pieces of the software break. A client may want to "bounce an idea off of you," when the reality is the responsible thing to do would be to bury your head in code.

This creates a dysfunctional spiral, where your day is so consumed by chores that you are robbed of the time that it would take to strategically organize the workload. It can be quite trapping without a clear way out. Sometimes you can let go of things that are deemed unimportant, but for things that are important (like filing taxes, preparing investor updates, or maintaining secure infrastructure), you just have to do them. And they take time.

The Timesheet Exercise has helped me in this situation. Here's how it works: pick a period of time you are going to study. I've done a week, two weeks, or a month, depending on the situation.

Then, draw a pie chart of how you think you will spend your time. Don't just do it in your head — actually draw it on paper or model it with fake data in spreadsheet software. Categorize each wedge of the pie based on the hat you are wearing for that task.

For example, you may be acting as a Bookkeeper, QA Tester, Product Manager, or Team Lead at various periods throughout the day.

Then make another pie chart of your ideal day. If you were focusing on all the things you felt you should be focusing on, how would you spend your day? Imagine for a moment that all the operational tasks that are bogging you down are addressed in some way (and don't worry about how just yet).

Next is to measure what the period of time actually looks like. During this time, act like you are an hourly worker and keep a timesheet. Log everything you do in the day, not just nine to five. Include things like breaks. I usually use Google Sheets.

Just like you did in the prediction, categorize each task based on the responsibility.

It's also a format that is more easily digested by others, so you can share the two pie charts with a co-founder, advisor, colleague, or friend and solicit ideas on moving from the actual pie to the ideal one.

At the end of the period, you compare the two. By being based on an actual timesheet, it filters out "recency bias" and you get an objective look at where you are spending your time.

Zach, you ask, what the heck is recency bias?

Let's take the James Cameron movie *Aliens* as an example. If you only watched the first half of the movie, you would swear that Bill Paxton is the star; he steals the show, and then dies about an hour in.

There's an hour left in the movie.

At the end, Sigourney Weaver has an epic final boss battle with the alien queen and wins. By that time, you forgot Bill Paxton was even in the movie. You remember Sigourney Weaver the most. That's recency bias.

And the Timesheet Exercise helps you get past it.

I have found that just telling trusted parties you are "too busy" and asking for help rarely leads to helpful results because the most recent event is usually top of mind and drowns out an objective measurement. This leads to a gripe session which can be therapeutic but doesn't really solve the problem.

Whereas with the pie chart approach, you can debate the merits of the allocation in the ideal chart, look at the undeniable data in the actual chart, and question what assumptions were wrong between the expected versus actual chart. The exercise forces you to focus on what really matters and what is really happening.

I do this exercise every six months, and I encourage my

team to do the same. It helps you view time more objectively, and in the end, all we really have is time.

19

EXERCISE: THE RESPONSIBILITY MAP

How do you determine the qualities of a healthy inner circle? You're in luck, I have an exercise for that, called the Responsibility Map. All it takes is a sheet of paper, pen or pencil, and about 30 minutes or so.

Start off assuming your company as you envision it is already successful in the market. What are the top disciplines your organization is world-class at? For Yembo, it was AI technology, SaaS distribution, and user interface design.

Each company will be different. For a bakery, it might be culinary excellence and distribution. For a fintech company, maybe it's cutting edge technology, compliance, and access to institutional capital.

Take some time to list out what your company needs. It's important to play a bit of fantasy thinking here — don't focus on where your startup is now (because there may not even be a company yet), imagine you are already successful and describe what you see.

Now, turn your list into a two-column table. In the second column, add in who will be filling this role. If the person is known, you can put their name. If not, list some résumé attributes a qualified person would have. This gives you a quantitative punch list of who you need to find to fill out your inner circle.

If you want some practice on this before making your own company's Responsibility Map, you can pick some well-known companies and go through the exercise for them. I prefer using publicly traded companies for this exercise since there are disclosure requirements and you can easily access information such as who the key executives are and how they are allocating their finances.

If you already have a co-founder, you can do the exercises independently, then compare after you both are done. You may find other perspectives clarify your thinking, challenge you, and help you identify gaps in your own reasoning. I've found it helpful to do this in a trial example before delving into the real exercise.

All of these responsibilities will need to be addressed, maybe not all right now, but on the way to the vision you had in mind when you started the exercise, you will need to account for these. If some responsibilities are not needed on day one, it's ok to prioritize the list and shorten it. At Yembo, we knew we needed sales leadership with expertise in software-as-a-service, but we also were cognizant of the fact that we didn't have anything to sell yet, so we decided to do sales ourselves as founders until we got the first million in annual recurring revenue, then focused on filling that gap afterward.

RESPONSIBILITY	OWNER
BUILD CORE AI TECH	SID
BUILD WEB PLATFORM	ZACH
MANAGE IP	ZACH
MANAGE SALES AND RENEWALS	SID (for now)
MOVING INDUSTRY EXPERTISE	TBD

The Responsibility Map exercise gives you a quantitative list of skills that your inner circle would need to have, but at the end of the day, living, breathing people are going to fill this role. In addition to assessing skills, it's helpful to assess personality traits as well. The more rigorous you are here, the easier it will be to fill the roles.

The first challenges you will face with the key people identified in your Map will likely be existential. Thinking these things through before you find yourself in the crunch of decision time is helpful.

20

MIND THE GAP

Your team's inner circle is not your inner circle.

The responsibility to set up a strong inner circle doesn't stop just with yourself as you put together the founding team. It also extends outward to the teams you will be putting together — maybe they are different engineering pods based on different product areas, customer success, sales, or design, to name a few options. As a founder you are not just responsible for your circle, but also for ensuring your employees have inner circles they can execute their goals with.

One factor affecting why employees decide to remain for longer periods of time is the quality of the team they are on.

Another is that employees can only have five or so strong relationships with colleagues in the workplace. At first this sounds unlikely, but think back to your past jobs.

Zooming in, the overall team quality is built out of individual relationships. This means that all key positions at a healthy, functioning organization should have strong relationships that accept, challenge, grow, and respect each other.

Yembo didn't have an official design team until 2020. We started off with the interface design being a responsibility handled by the frontend engineering team. This worked well enough to get our initial product launched, but after a few years, the limitations started to show.

From an outsider's perspective, it manifested itself in our team slowly losing their ability to iterate to make clients happy in their surveys.

We shipped our first version of the product as soon as we possibly could. The product was barely viable when we started getting feedback and testing it out with our initial set of clients. This got us in the habit of listening to customer feedback and incorporating it into our weekly software updates.

Inevitably, we shipped all the easy improvements. We were left with conflicting ideas of what direction we could go in next. Clients mentioned certain features were not intuitive.

Or, worse, they were not using the product at all.

When we checked our feedback backlog in our project management tool, we found there wasn't a clear set of things to do to remedy the situation.

What changed? The main discovery was that the key people working on this problem were no longer Sid and me.

A new group of employees were now involved, and they didn't have the same Responsibility Map that we had. So whereas we could fall back on our founder peers, advisors, investors, and others in our network with questions on things we hadn't encountered before, the newer employees didn't have this infrastructure.

When I sketched out the Responsibility Map for the existing team, the gaps became obvious:

RESPONSIBILITY	OWNER
GATHER CUSTOMER FEEDBACK	CUSTOMER SUCCESS
GENERATE PRODUCT REQUIREMENTS	CUSTOMER SUCCESS
BUILD PROTOTYPES	TBD
USABILITY STUDIES	TBD
IMPLEMENTATION	ENGINEERING
QA	ENGINEERING
RELEASE	ENGINEERING

The nature of our problems had evolved, but the team tasked with solving them wasn't properly equipped to handle them. In our early days, we needed to prove that AI technology could work effectively and reliably. Once we achieved that, we encountered a hornet's nest of usability problems to resolve.

Whenever things are not working as smoothly or quickly as you'd like, it can be helpful to draw a new Responsibility Map and see where the unmet responsibilities lie.

In our case, this led to up-skilling one of our frontend engineers to become a designer. This added to her skill stack, and helped us fill in the unmet needs in the Responsibility Map. Win-win.

The Responsibility Map framework ensured we thought through the scenario before making any major changes.

21

THE DANGERS OF FEEDBACK

I n Eric Ries' seminal work, *The Lean Startup*, founders are encouraged to build a Minimum Viable Product (MVP) as quickly as they can, then measure based on feedback, learn based on interpretations of the feedback, and build again based on those learnings.[1] This build-measure-learn feedback loop encourages finding product-market fit because it relies on shipping often, showing the outside world the product, and interpreting their feedback.

The concept struck a chord — the book launched in 2011 and by 2018 had surpassed one million copies sold and had been translated into over 30 languages. As with any book at that scale, it received critiques both in favor and opposed.

I've found one area to stand out as the most crucial when evaluating the build-measure-learn process for a project — handling feedback.

The problem with feedback is everyone seems to have an opinion. Whether or not the feedback is valuable is another matter entirely.

Next time you're in a room with 10 or more people, if you

ask how to solve a challenging problem such as income inequality or climate change, you may get a few blank stares. This is because these problems are challenging and people generally understand their area of expertise may fall outside of what skills they believe are required to solve such a problem.

Now take the same room with the same people but this time, ask them to critique something — what could be improved about the catering? What looks wrong with this logo concept? What do you think of this playlist?

Suddenly, everyone has an opinion.

If we don't want to be like the Paranoid Android whose "opinion is of no consequence at all," what can we do to give good feedback? Or at least improve ours?

Good feedback is mindful of the context that it lives within — the goals, impact, and conviction/experience curve (which we will cover more about in the next chapter). Below is the framework I provide to my direct reports on providing me with feedback when plans we have charted out together have changed:

1. **Here's the situation** — Summarize what the original plan was, what happened to interrupt the plan, and why it requires attention.
2. **Here's what I'd do** — Recognizing that it's easier to critique than create, prepare a proposal for review and feedback.
3. **Here's why I'd do that** — The feedback giver may have more context into the problem than the recipient, so explain the thought process. This allows the recipient to get a fuller picture and gives the ability to incorporate pieces of the

advice even if the entire plan isn't adopted wholesale.

4. **Here's what I need you for** — Make it clear what you'd like the other party to do, and if it's not immediately apparent, the timeframe the recipient is expected to act on.

It's been my experience that this approach works with many business relationships, not just managers. It can be applied in any relationship where feedback is being given or solicited — co-founders, peers, or investors. (Your mileage may vary if you try this on a spouse or partner).

As a side note, the World Wide Web Consortium (W3C), the standards body behind web browser technology, solicits input from the general public on proposed new features for the web.[2] They have an amazing template on how to solicit feedback on a proposed idea. It may be wise to borrow from their approach, since it works at Internet scale, which is one of the largest human institutions the world has ever seen.

As a founder you cannot control the amount of feedback you get in a given day. But with the right framework for evaluating, you can be reasonably confident that the right mix is occupying your mental capacity.

In order to effectively create an idea that others deem viable, many details need to be sorted out.

On the other hand, in order to critique an idea, just one problem needs to be raised.

It is far easier to critique something than to create, which is why feedback is so easy to come by, but practical suggestions that solve problems are more elusive.

Given that feedback is so prevalent, an effective founder will be adept at identifying good feedback.

Oftentimes feedback is forced upon founders — it is not always solicited. Feedback can come in the form of an unexpected rejection during a contract negotiation, or a sales deal getting pushed another quarter for budgetary reasons.

Whether solicited or not, having a framework for evaluating and acting on feedback is key. Done right, it allows for leveraging someone else's insights into making the company better.

Opinions *are* of consequence.

22

LOW PASS FILTER

But there's a catch.

Giving and receiving feedback are not two equal entities.

It is generally much easier to give feedback than to receive it well.

For example, consider a sales prospect backing out of a deal. "It's too expensive! My CFO will not allow a purchase of this size outside of the fiscal planning process," he may say.

Deciding what to do next is a much more complex task:

- Do we simply mark the opportunity as closed/lost in the Customer Relationship Manager (CRM), with a note to follow back up at the end of the fiscal year?
- Do we treat the feedback with suspicion and ask more questions to dig into the real reason?
- Are there product deficiencies, and resolving them would have changed the outcome?

As founders we receive signals constantly. A diligent founder will use time wisely, and recognize that it takes much more energy and time to receive feedback than to give it.

A framework for evaluation is useful to ensure that the most pressing goals are getting the attention they deserve.

What decision will be made from this feedback? Is it easily reversible? If so, perhaps it's acceptable to spend less time culling the feedback. Is it a bet-the-farm type of scenario?

Then perhaps it's better to get more data points before making the decision. Second opinions are common in the medical industry, and they are equally as valuable in the startup world.

You don't have to really listen to it all, but you can get a real sense of things by applying what is known in audio as a low pass filter. In an interview, music pioneer Brian Eno describes this tool:[1]

I started experimenting with my favorite tool of all in the studio which is the low-pass filter, in other words, just taking off all the high frequency of things has an amazing psychological effect. It creates scale distance, warmth, and a weird sort of intimacy which is quite strange.

I think because you're missing a lot of detail your brain very actively engages with those kinds of sounds. So I started thinking perhaps there could be a kind of music like that where we take existing songs, you know like a Rihanna record and we just put it through a low-pass filter so nothing above 250 hertz is audible. Then it sounds like you're listening to a song being played in another room.

> So then if you listen to a Rihanna record through a wall it's not exhausting, it's warm, but you get the gist of it.

Feedback is also an audio engineering term, so apply a low pass filter to your feedback to get a general sense of things, but not be bombarded and numbed by detail (higher frequencies in Eno's example).

A person giving the feedback is a human being, with skills, desires, ambitions, strengths, and weaknesses. They will have areas they are strong at and other areas where their knowledge is limited.

For example, an investor with a background in starting SaaS companies might have valuable business model ideas and pricing advice for a startup. But their opinion in terms of how to design the software is outside their expertise.

It's important not to necessarily accept or reject feedback depending on the source.

In general, when soliciting feedback, the easiest kind to digest is from an expert in their field speaking with high conviction:

EXPERTISE

		LOW	HIGH
CONVICTION	LOW	SALES PROSPECT PASSES, NOT A GOOD FIT	A SAVVY INVESTOR WALKS FROM THE DEAL
	HIGH	AN ASPIRING ENGINEER APPLIES FOR THEIR FIRST SOFTWARE JOB	A PASSIONATE CUSTOMER WANTS TO BE THE FIRST TO MARKET

The problem is, feedback comes all over the spectrum. Uncovering motives plays a part in this process. The sales prospect might just want to get off the call, so their conviction about what you need to do to improve your product may be low.

Whereas an investor whose family member tried out the product might feel strongly about how the interface could be improved, but the advice is coming from someone who doesn't have much experience designing interfaces.

Due to these factors, it's important to not accept or reject feedback solely from the expertise of the giver of the feedback. But it is helpful to understand that not all feedback is created equal, accepting one course of action implicitly rejects another. At the end of the day, the buck stops at you, so you need to be able to stand behind your own decision.

23

EXERCISE: THE ONLY YOU TEST

It's not in my nature to delegate. Learning how to do so is absolutely a skill. How did I get into a situation where I literally had to learn how to delegate?

For me, and I imagine a lot of people who start companies, at first, a startup is a side project. It takes up maybe five hours a week, then 10 hours a week, and then it gradually grows and grows. At some point along the way, delegation becomes a necessity because eventually, you run out of time in your day. I think most people understand this much. But where things get complicated is in choosing what to delegate, and how to do it well.

In school, I was the kind of student who disliked group projects because they usually entailed doing the work of four people myself, then begrudging the freeloaders when we all got an "A" grade. In hindsight, I don't think I was the most fun student to be around.

At the time, I felt like nobody cared as much as I did. As an adult, I can now see that poor delegation on my part was to blame.

As I've related, at Yembo, we initially started with remote workers. We had a team in India and a team in Ukraine, and to keep them busy you constantly give them work. Which means you're always having to think things through and spec it out.

The challenge I was running into is when you are giving yourself work, you just inherently know what to do. You've been there since day one, you've built it from the ground up.

But if your startup is gaining any momentum, there comes a point when you can't do everything anymore, and you must offload tasks that you could do on your own, but you just don't have the time anymore. It's a matter of giving in and sending the work to someone else even if you don't feel as though you need to.

I've gotten into hot water a few times during our fundraising. Since I was not delegating properly, I couldn't effectively distribute the work. Since Yembo started, we have done weekly software releases on Wednesdays. Startups need to ship fast to keep customers happy and incorporate their feedback, so I was unwavering in this belief.

The problem was, shipping every week implies that new features are ready to ship each week, and the testing process can keep up.

When the product is very simple, this is not an issue and delegation can be considered optional. At the point in the company's trajectory where we were doing around a million dollars in annual revenue, the lack of delegation became a problem. I was trying to work on the features going into the weekly releases, handle our QA process, monitor the servers and fix any issues that cropped up, all at the same time I was needed for fundraising.

In the startup world, fundraising is essential. Something

had to give, but giving away any one responsibility on my plate would have had catastrophic consequences for the business.

When we were raising our seed round, we had a meeting where prospective investors flew down from Seattle to visit us in San Diego. They showed up at the office about half an hour early. Sid and I had planned to take them out to lunch.

I was working on a feature that was almost complete, but I was still doing some testing to make sure everything worked well. Even though the investors only arrived about 30 minutes early, I saw the domino chain that it was going to kick off — if I didn't finish the testing before the lunch, it'd interrupt a delicate chain of tasks I had lined up for myself for the rest of the day.

But the fundraising needed to be done.

So I rushed the QA process and pushed the feature live. The rollout succeeded, so we went to lunch and talked about the future of the business we were building.

Every chance I got, I'd quietly check my phone for support tickets or crash reports, trying to be discreet each time I peeked.

Predictably, the new feature had a defect, and certain customers weren't able to upload videos anymore due to an authentication error. A couple of support tickets trickled in.

I tried to follow the thread of the lunch conversation while mentally trying to troubleshoot where the bug was. This effectively reduced me to grinning and nodding my head at the ends of people's sentences. Sid picked up that something was wrong and asked if I needed to get back to something. The investors were gracious and understanding, so we wrapped up early, and I went back to my desk before our afternoon meeting to fix the bug properly.

Before I properly learned to delegate, these kinds of stories were not entirely rare. If I had to estimate, about 30% of releases needed to be rolled back in one way or another to be properly fixed before going out again.

Ironically, at the same time, I believed I couldn't offload QA onto anyone else, despite my track record being so poor. We didn't have that many customers at the time, but the ones that we did have depended on us, so what's a conscientious founder to do? Spend my time keeping the lights on, or do I pause all that to fundraise?

I wished I could clone myself and do both.

This is where a decision-making framework can help resolve the dilemma. I prefer a simple test, one I call the Only You test. When someone feels they cannot delegate tasks, there is often a laundry list of things to be done, and the context required to execute the tasks is so specific that it's considered to be too burdensome to try to offload the work.

The Only You test remedies this situation, and it's simple to carry out.

To do it, write down the tasks you have on your plate. Assume everything on the list genuinely needs to be handled, or some unspeakably bleak future becomes reality.

Now, look at the laundry list of tasks listed in front of you. Add a note explaining what skills are needed to carry out each task well. The more specific, the better.

With the table laid out in front of you, question which tasks can only be done by you. That means if anyone else were to try to do that task, it would materially suffer. In these cases, only you can do the task correctly. Here's my Only You test I made when I was in this situation:

TASK	SKILLS	ONLY ME ?
PRODUCT ROADMAP PLANNING	PRODUCT UNDERSTANDING, TECH SKILLS, VISION	YES
FEATURE BUILDING	REACT, JS, PHP, MONGO DB, AWS, CSS	NO
TESTING	PRODUCT FUNCTIONALITY EXPECTATIONS	NO
MAINTAINING INFRA	AWS, IT SKILLS	NO
PEOPLE MANAGMENT	EMPATHY, VISION, MENTORING	YES
FUNDRAISING	COMMUNICATION, VISION, MARKET UNDERSTANDING	YES

This exercise helps focus on what tasks can genuinely only be done by you and which ones you are only temporarily filling because you haven't found a way to properly offload yet.

This filter allows you to learn how to let things go and let others handle some of the work that initially you felt only you could do. And it may change over time.

As an example, our roadmap planning could not have been effectively offloaded when we were a team of seven people with a handful of customers, but around becoming a team of 30, we did start having others make product roadmaps at the company.

The Only You test is meant to be a snapshot at a particular point in time, not a universal truth.

24

THE POWER OF PROCESS

It was around 7 a.m. and I was getting ready to head into the office. While I was packing up, my phone buzzed with an incoming text. It was Ken, one of our first customers at Yembo.

If there is such a thing as an ideal early customer, it was embodied in Ken. He was super positive, high energy, motivated us to ship fast, and celebrated his team's wins with us. And ship fast, we did. Often at the expense of reliability. Hence the incoming text message.

> Hey bud, when you get a minute could you check what's going on with Yembo?

It was perhaps the calmest and most polite way to mention something rather dire.

One of our team members had released a bug into production. The way the bug affected things, it would crash while trying to process a video. And since the processing crashed, the system would try again. But then the retry would also crash because of the bug.

So the system would try again. So on and so forth, until the only thing the backend is doing is crashing, and none of the videos being uploaded were being processed. No data was lost, but everything uploaded in the previous hour was stuck in limbo.

I flipped open my laptop and checked out what was going on. I fixed the issue and reported back.

> Good morning Ken — try now. I just pushed up a fix.

Thanks buddy!

The issue was resolved and all the pending estimates were able to be delivered.

But internally, I knew the systematic problem was still present.

The problem was, the scenario that led to the bug could very well happen again. The QA process was not mature to effectively test release candidates before they went live.

We were relying on our customers to be our testers, using the support channels to report bugs to us. Not ideal.

The engineer who made the bug played no part in the resolution because I didn't have time to loop him in.

By turning myself into a superhero who drops everything to resolve the issue, I was robbing the people I really needed to be able to do the work of the opportunity to learn what it takes to operate their deliverables.

It can be tempting to move on after the immediate issue has been resolved. The mantra of "this too shall pass" generally applies to every situation on a long enough time horizon.

I've found that most issues that crop up end up not being

big deals in the grand scheme of things. The ones that present themselves as the most urgent often mask the genuine underlying issue.

In this case, the skillset I needed to extinguish the current problem was a backend engineer with troubleshooting abilities. But by exercising these skills myself, I prevented the QA tester and the backend engineer who caused the issue from understanding how the overall process works.

In a sense, by being diligent and responding to the customer's request, I had inadvertently influenced the company culture that deprived the engineers of ownership.

If an engineer contributes code that causes problems, and someone else will come in and clean it up, the engineer may not even know their code caused a problem. So the next time they build something, they don't know the pitfalls to avoid and are likely to cause similar problems again.

Even with the best of intentions, a suboptimal process will cause unnecessary anxiety and tension between the "doer/breaker" and the "responsible fixer."

Fortunately, we didn't let this situation fester for long. To solve the problem, we made a few process improvements. Note how the fundamental skillset required in the proper fix is different than the one that was required to put out the fire:

- We set up a way for proposed code changes to be tested before they were accepted into the overall codebase.
- We developed a process for our engineering ticketing system to hold testing instructions, so the engineer working on the feature could explain to the testing team scenarios they could think of that should be verified.

- We set up an internal checklist of scenarios that should be tested before the code goes live, so we can have confidence that the end-to-end system works well before releasing it to real customers.
- We configured automatic monitoring and alerting, so if anything were to slip through the cracks, we'd be proactively notified by the infrastructure instead of relying on texts from customers.
- We set up an incident reporting system, so for any issues that did affect real customers, we'd dispassionately examine the situation, identify what went wrong, how it was resolved, and what process improvements could be made. This allowed even engineers who were not involved in the particular incident to learn from the situation in a low-pressure way after the problem had been resolved.

After these changes were made, several benefits emerged:

- Code quality metrics improved. By having more stringent quality requirements as a criterion for admission to the codebase, problems were caught in low-stress situations before they affected customers.
- Engineers became more autonomous, since they had visibility into what kinds of problems were happening with their code, and could learn from them.
- Releases became less dramatic. Where they used to take a team of three to four people six to eight hours on average of manual testing, patching, and

rolling back when things went wrong, they became something one engineer could do in 15 minutes.
- The alerting gave engineers peace of mind that someone was watching and making sure things were humming along smoothly.

The overall lesson is to be mindful of the fact that lots of fires and urgent matters crop up during the day. Take some time to analyze the situation and pinpoint where the real problem is.

Oftentimes the real problem is hidden several layers below the obvious ones. It can be helpful to start with open-ended questions like "Why is this situation happening?" and "What would need to be in place to prevent this from escalating to my desk in the future?"

Do not underestimate the power of process.

Lesson Learned: The exact same team — all the skillsets, personalities, and ambitions can either execute dysfunctionally or exceptionally. The dividing line is dictated by process.

PART IV

GROWING TEAMS

"Fitter happier / More productive"

Fitter Happier • Radiohead • OK Computer

25

FINDING A CO-FOUNDER

C oworkers are a significant component of a job's attractiveness, the company's performance, and the reason employees choose to stay at or leave a company.

In most companies, the employee's boss will assign them to a project, and the project has a team working on it.

The employee will spend significant time and energy working with the colleagues on the team. Still, generally with individual contributor positions, the employee themself has very little say in who those colleagues are.

It is instructive to think through how inner circles work, how to select a good one, and how to build a company with solid teams throughout the organization.

Like many things in startup life, selecting colleagues presents both an opportunity and a responsibility.

In a startup, your inner circle — the group of people you spend the most time with — is something that you can decide.

The proper selection can make the company succeed

beyond expectations. The wrong one can drive things into the ground.

Your founding team is perhaps the most consequential decision of your inner circle. The proverbial deck is stacked against startups in many ways — finding product/market fit, getting your first customers, finding funding through sales, consulting work, or outside investment.

If, as a founder, you also have the burden of an inner circle you can't trust or rely on, the entire company is at risk.

Many startups have a founding team as opposed to a single founder. There is no singular path to success, but looking broadly, most startups have multiple founders. A 2021 study found in the group of startups studied, the average number of founders was 2.3.[1]

A co-founder can provide a unique perspective to crucial business decisions, especially if they have a different background from the other founders. Operationally, they can manage different areas of the business.

For me when I was starting Yembo, I was confident in my skills as a software engineer but felt I was lacking in core AI experience. I decided the co-founder path was the right one to take.

There are multiple ways you can find a co-founder.

Maybe you have an idea and attend networking or industry events to find a co-founder.

Maybe you already know your co-founder(s) and are looking for the right problem to solve together with your skillsets.

However you find your founding team, selecting them based on how they perform under pressure is helpful. Lots of people present well, but a co-founder relationship is different.

There is pressure to deliver, or the whole organization comes crashing down.

Often the first investors are close with the founding team. Hence, the added stress of failure in business can be a personal letdown to the founder's most influential connections.

Moreover, founders are socially expected to be upbeat and optimistic. So, you'll need to handle these challenges with a smile. Some people can't healthily manage that amount of stress. This is why it's helpful to evaluate based on how the person handles themselves under pressure.

Here are a few of the questions my co-founder Sid and I discussed before we signed the incorporation documents:

- What does your wife think?
- How long can you go without a salary?
- What are your thoughts on us both having admin access to our company's bank accounts and credit cards?
- What is the most stressful situation you have handled professionally?
- What are you proud of regarding the way you handled things? What do you wish you had done differently?
- What does your wife think?

I wouldn't categorize any of these conversations as fun. They get at a person's character, not just the areas they are meant to deliver.

But these conversations must be had. You are tying your economic futures together.

Please do yourself a favor and don't skip the conversation because it's uncomfortable.

You will have plenty of real challenges ahead — these sorts of conversations and ground rules that may result from them are much easier to have in the abstract when there is no immediate problem.

On several occasions, founder friends asked me for advice after their co-founder made a dramatic move like revoking access to the company bank account or digging into an inability to agree on who would take the CEO title.

These are challenging but necessary conversations — have them before you're in the thick of things.

26

LEARNING TO MANAGE PEOPLE

The early stages of a company are defined by significant change. The budding company searches for product/market fit, and plans can change from week to week or even day to day. Often, companies start with just an idea, but the hard work of building a customer base willing to pay for the product lies ahead.

Even corporate spin-offs or companies that start in consulting undergo a similar process as they aim to productize and scale their offerings. In order to be responsive to market feedback, plans need to be flexible. Since the stakes are often existential, agility is a necessity.

To reach a mature phase, a company must first undergo an almost magical chapter of growth. In this phase, where the company is building, attracting its first customers, listening to feedback, and scaling out the product to make it more widely applicable to other clients, employees often get to do some of their careers' best work.

The company is generally small, everyone understands the mission, and knows what they need to do to help the company get there. Processes haven't yet been bogged down by bureaucracy. For those who can withstand some ambiguity and flexibility in plans, it can be quite a productive environment.

Finding yourself at a company in this phase is a matter of being in the right place at the right time. Often, being in the right place at the right time is attributed to good fortune.

The flip side of being at the right place at the right time is how circumstances can change.

One does not need to look far to find horror stories of early interpersonal dynamics failing as the company matures — the co-founder who couldn't scale and needed to be replaced, or the early investor who wanted to take the company in a different direction.

However, reality is much more layered and nuanced than a simplistic view that the company is a rocket ship that outgrows certain people who cannot keep up. Enter Rachel Ruderman.

Rachel was the first software engineer I hired at Yembo, despite her reservations about applying the title to herself. She joined Yembo in 2017 and built significant portions of the company's first product over the next three years.

At first glance, Rachel's career trajectory didn't resemble that of a typical software engineer. Her background was in translation; she held a Master's in translation from a Spanish university, and she had worked for three years in the translation industry in Spain.

In 2017, without a clear picture of where things would lead, Rachel enrolled in a coding bootcamp. At the time, she refused to refer to herself as a software engineer, preferring the term "web developer" because "a software engineer carries a different connotation. It has a different weight to it."

Unlike lawyers, doctors, or architects, there is no academic credential that deems someone a software engineer. However, years of social conditioning can take time to overcome.

We were laser-focused on making the AI technology work, and our only open positions at the time were for computer vision engineers to build perception and mapping technology from a video feed.

When I first met her, I was impressed with the professional persistence she exhibited by literally willing the meeting into existence. Before I even had a chance to think about putting the job posting together, Rachel had effectively taken the job off the market. Sometimes, positioning yourself in the right place at the right time appears as luck to outsiders but requires courage and a healthy disregard of the fear of rejection.

It took Yembo about three months to get the first 100 end customers through the system. A year later, we routinely got our 100th unique customer by 11 a.m. each morning. But as the company grew, our team and our processes needed to grow as well.

Unfortunately, the early glory days had to transition to something more scalable. The era of "cowboy coding," or recklessly shipping untested features in the name of moving fast, had to come to a close.

I was no longer able to invest much time working with Rachel. I needed a specific outcome by a certain time to meet a deadline for one of our larger enterprise contracts.

As I confessed to my wife one night after a particularly demanding day, "For most of my career, I feel I've done a pretty good job. But now I feel like a C- student in all the areas that matter."

I had too many responsibilities that I no longer had much time to work alongside Rachel and discuss pros and cons of the software design she was working on. She needed someone to bounce ideas off of, but I had too many responsibilities so I couldn't fill that role myself. Our conversations focused more around deadlines and less on software architecture. The company was still so small that there wasn't anyone else who could fill this role for her. As a result, I failed to provide an environment where Rachel's skills could shine. That failure cost us a great employee.

Just like companies change, people's needs also change. Rachel had progressed beyond the point where she needed syntax help in building products. She was ready to take on the next level of responsibility, but I was too tied up in business matters to be the technical lead she needed.

I don't believe in the Karma Police, but I do believe in supporting people who have supported me. When Rachel decided to leave, she had a contracting opportunity but nothing long term yet. We gratefully gave her a laptop so she'd be able to continue coding if she had downtime between gigs.

At the end of the day, who knows? Maybe a great employee who needed to move on will come back.

27

STARTUP FOLK: RACHEL IN HER OWN WORDS

A s I was writing this book, it occurred to me that it could be valuable to share the perspective of a few people whom I have worked with at Yembo. The book has several chapters titled "Startup Folk," where an individual is given an opportunity to tell the Yembo story from their perspective. Each person featured in such a chapter tenured at Yembo for at least two years and made significant product contributions, so their opinions are of consequence. The interviews were lightly edited for clarity and are reproduced in this book with their consent.

How did you arrive at Yembo?

My time at Yembo started with a cold LinkedIn message in 2017. It was actually my second message to Zach; the first went unnoticed a few weeks earlier with my connect request on LinkedIn. We had never met, we had never corresponded, but his LinkedIn headline said "We're hiring!" and I was most certainly looking:

SEP 22, 2017

Rachel Ruderman - Software Engineer · 11:29 AM

Hi Zach! I saw that you're hiring and I was wondering if you have any junior web developer roles available? Thanks :)

Zach Rattner · 12:05 PM

Hi Rachel, thanks for reaching out. We don't have any web development roles open right now, but we'll have more web work coming up in the coming weeks/months and are thinking about taking in another dev then. If you're interested in an informational interview to learn more about us and show me what you're working on, I'd be happy to chat more. No pressure either way though!

A few months earlier I had completed a full-stack JavaScript coding bootcamp and I was looking for my first gig. Over the years, people had mentioned I should try coding, but I always shied away from the idea, thinking it was for math and science types. Then, an opportunity arose to enroll in a coding bootcamp at a steep discount, and I was amazed to discover what a highly creative and expressive field it is. It was like a whole new world opened up to me, a world where I could create anything.

Zach explained that Yembo did not have any current openings for my role, but offered to meet up nonetheless. We met later that day at a Starbucks. I remember my first impression was that he was humble, down-to-earth, and not at all like the last startup founder I met, who wanted me to work three months for free in a "time for experience" scheme. It was a great meeting. Zach told me about the vision for Yembo, I showed him the tutorial projects I was working on, and I walked away feeling refreshed that, although he didn't have an opening for me, there were honest employers out there.

Now imagine my absolute shock when just a week later I was offered contract work for Yembo. I was baffled. It took months for me to work up the courage to ask, "How did that happen?" Looking back, I understand now that Zach saw more in me than I saw in myself. In my tutorial projects, he saw initiative. In my LinkedIn messages and willingness to meet at the drop of a hat, he saw persistence. He was reading between the lines.

Did you ever feel impostor syndrome?

Starting out, I didn't feel the impostor syndrome that typically afflicts career switchers and minorities in tech. I attribute that to two reasons:

Firstly, Yembo was great at meeting me where I was at. I never met a challenge I didn't ultimately learn the answer to thanks to Zach and, if he didn't know himself, he'd manage to find a contractor online who could educate us. This was so empowering when it came to taking risks. If I had an idea, and Zach liked it, it didn't matter if I didn't know how to figure it out 100% myself. We would hire someone to fill the gaps and make the impossible possible. At Yembo I was never limited by my own limitations.

Secondly, my years of language learning taught me to have grace with myself. When you're learning a spoken language, you will sound silly. Particularly in Spanish, you're going to tell people you're pregnant (embarazada) when you mean to say you're embarrassed. But then one day, you'll dream in that language and speak without thinking. The early fumbles are an integral part of the process. It all comes together with time.

What is one of your favorite moments at Yembo?

One of my shining moments at Yembo happened when we landed our first international customer and they needed the app translated. When you switch careers people talk about starting over, but you're not actually starting over. You have all these transferrable skills waiting to be unleashed in new ways. Not only was I able to draw on my previous experience to coordinate the international translation project, but I was able to use my newfound coding skills to automate parts of the process. It was a dream come true.

What was leaving Yembo like?

My glory days at Yembo began to fade as the company grew. Because of my background in quality control, I was so focused on code quality I overlooked the crucial importance of a healthy team dynamic. We faced classic issues like scope creep due to lack of project management. And ultimately there came a point where I felt I was the foremost frontend expert in the room, but I was lacking in experience myself. I was making architectural decisions that I knew were problematic, and I needed someone with more experience to provide feedback. Without that resource, I felt like the blind leading the blind.

In the years since I have always rooted for Yembo and I love to see the company updates. I look back fondly on my time there. It was a place of limitless exploration. I could follow anywhere my curiosity piqued: frontend, AWS, automation scripts, testing, translation. It was a playground for my mind.

It's been an impressive first five years, I can't wait to see what Yembo comes up with next.

28

AS SMALL AS POSSIBLE

A nother constraint we had was space. Physical space, not outer space. That's Elon's purview.

Our first office was a back room subleased from my real estate agent who operated the moving company. The moving company was great for getting direct feedback because we were literally sharing office space. If someone complained about the product, I'd hear it.

The building was a converted food storage facility — I was told our particular room was previously used to prepare muffins and other pastries to be sold to grocery stores. The room had high industrial ceilings that gave a cavernous feeling even though the space was actually only 200 square feet.

Since the room wasn't being used before we moved in, it was pretty barebones — a bare concrete floor, no lighting, and a single window that didn't open.

But the office didn't need to be anything special — it was *our* office. I loved it.

We installed our own carpet and I obsessed over the different options, ultimately settling for the least expensive one. We put up a huge whiteboard. I bought a lamp to take care of the lack of lighting. Turns out a single lamp wasn't sufficient to light the space, so I bought eight more and put them around the perimeter of the room. It gave the room a Polynesian tiki torch vibe. I thought it was cool. I don't know if anyone else did.

Sid and I realized we weren't going to be able to compete against fancy tech office amenities, so we didn't bother trying. We ensured people had what they needed — desks, chairs, Wi-Fi, snacks, health insurance, but we didn't care if things weren't flashy. If flashiness was important to a candidate, we felt they weren't a good fit for the stage of the company we were at.

When superstar Hollywood agent Michael Ovitz and his partners started Creative Artists Agency, they borrowed $21,000 from a bank, rented a tiny office, conducted all their business on card tables, and furnished the space with folding chairs from home.[1] CAA ultimately grew into one of the largest and most powerful forces in Hollywood. They didn't need Herman Miller chairs. There's a lesson there.

Our product probably would never have gotten off the ground if it wasn't for that initial space. We hired our first three employees there, and everyone worked in the same room. We had one goal we were all working on — a working end-to-end product where:

- The mover could send an invite link to the customer,
- The customer clicks the link and scans quick videos of each room in their house, and
- The AI processes the videos and shows the results to the mover.

Collaboration came so easily we almost took it for granted. With only five people, everyone knew what everyone else was working on. And in such close quarters, if anyone had a question or wanted to brainstorm or have a code review, they could literally swivel their chair around and tap the other person on the shoulder.

Ultimately we grew out of the space — the fire code said we couldn't add any more people so we had to get a larger office. But the lessons we learned on collaboration still stick with us to this day:

1) Have as small of a team as is viable to build a new product.

Each additional person adds complexity to the relationship graph:

- Two people: one relationship between A and B
- Three people: three relationships: A and B, B and C, A and C
- Four people: six relationships: A and B, A and C, A and D, B and C, B and D, C and D
- 10 people: 45 relationships. Yikes.

If just one relationship is contentious, it affects the whole group and can stifle progress. Collaborating is simply easier with smaller teams.

There is such a thing as too small — e.g., if certain disciplines are required but not staffed, or if there is too much work for a particular discipline to carry out, but the principle still stands.

Jeff Bezos also does this with the Two Pizza Rule, which

states that the ideal team size working on a problem can be fed by two pizzas.[2] The wildcard here is how much each engineer likes pizza.

2) Communicate openly.

In the early days, we were moving so fast because we hadn't yet proven that customers would pay for this product. We were impatiently and restlessly hurtling toward this goal. Otherwise, Yembo would just be an expensive hobby, not a viable business. I wrote code that had bugs, and things crashed, but boy did we move fast.

With some employees who have joined later, I noticed a hesitancy to speak candidly when the feedback was critical. It's easy to heap praises but if something isn't working well, it can be challenging to "poke the bear" and say so. In the early days we got this psychological safety that folks felt comfortable saying when things weren't working.

"Zach, I broke your API" was not an uncommon phrase spoken. There was nothing punitive or judgmental about it — just a byproduct of moving fast.

3) Spend time together.

When the team was this small, we'd do just about everything together. We'd have lunch, go on walks to take a brain break, and work alongside each other. This paid off in the form of people just "getting it" when we were working on solving problems. Almost to an uncanny degree. I once could tell that I had shipped an API change with an issue just by reading the look on the frontend engineer's face.

There is a problem in physics, specifically gravitational

physics, known as the "Three Body Problem". I'm going to butcher it here for the sake of an analogy.

When you have two gravitational bodies, such as the sun and the moon, it's very easy to calculate their orbits. They both have mass and you just run the math.

Interestingly, when a third body is added in, such as earth, the problem becomes much more difficult to solve, to the point that you really can't get a predictable answer.

So adding just one extra variable causes a certain type of chaos.

The same is true with people in a room. There is a certain vibe when two people are working in a room, but when you add a third person, things change.

When you add a fourth person, they change more. This is what I meant by talking about the relationship graph.

Smaller can be better at a startup when dealing with teams. It allows focus and can hold chaos at bay.

29

THE TIME WARP PAYS OFF

W e knew we needed to invest heavily in AI technology, which was our ticket to relevance. If we didn't have a functional AI system with the ability to learn from all the data coming in, we wouldn't have a path to a viable business. This meant that in the early days when budget was limited, we prioritized hiring AI engineers. As a result, I was handling the software engineering side of things not immediately related to AI: database design, APIs, frontend, and 15 other things.

There came a point, before there were significant resources available, where I wanted some software help. Not AI talent, but someone who could help me build the UI and business logic that went around the AI.

And since we didn't have many paying customers yet, I had to pay for this help out of pocket. Naturally, I was looking for talent in lower cost areas than San Diego (that would be the entire rest of the world) and ended up finding amazing talent in India and Ukraine.

The individual freelancers I found in each country were great. I ended up hiring more of them as Yembo scaled, to the point where both are now regional leads. When engineers join the team, many mention it seems obvious to have remote teams in staggered time zones to make continual progress. But it all came to be from a resource constraint in the early days that turned out to be a blessing in disguise.

In very unexpected ways.

It was the fall of 2017, and my co-founder and I were at dinner with a significant client with expansion potential. Their CIO was talking about the future of the company and the different areas where we might be able to collaborate together. Things went off to a great start (or so I thought), but then he veered into a laundry list of feature gaps that our product had. None of the feature gaps were news to me, but I had underestimated the urgency.

We had spent so much of our time and energy on improving the AI that we weren't as focused on the smaller features that folks had been asking for us to add into our software. As it turns out, business clients care about outcomes more than using shiny AI technology, so these little things were adding up.

I excused myself from the table to go to the restroom. Once out of sight, I messaged our lead engineer in India. I quickly explained the top issues that seemed to be most pressing, i.e. those that he could knock out quickly. His day was just starting, and I had grabbed him just in time. I headed back to the table, acted like nothing special had happened. But I knew that progress was being made.

The next morning I woke up around 7 a.m., reviewed the changes and released them. We met back at the client's offices around 9 a.m. Several of the engineers were surprised at how quickly we had addressed their concerns.

Let's do the time warp again!

If I had infinite resources from day one, I would have opted to have a larger team in San Diego. This would have likely made progress easier and faster to get things off the ground, but we would have missed out on the benefits that come from distributing the team.

And what tools do I use to manage teams worldwide and get things done?

- GitHub for source control. Every change requires a pull request.
- Jira for ticketing. Use their automation to link GitHub pull requests with Jira tickets.
- Slack for asynchronous communication. I have a template for end-of-day reports which covers the tasks that were worked on that day and what the plans for the next day are. This is helpful when coordinating across time zones and the reports come in throughout the day from various people. We've had more success with EOD reports than a daily standup meeting.
- Postman for APIs. Whenever an API is created or changed, the corresponding Postman entry is updated too.
- Figma for representing the design. Comments are dropped on each UI element explaining the API that is called. This makes it unambiguous what the interface between the frontend and backend should be.

- Clocker app for tracking time in different locations.
- Coffee. Lots of coffee.

Lesson Learned: While time zones can present challenges, they can be used to your advantage when leveraged properly.

30

CELEBRATING WINS

There is a common temptation to focus on what's wrong in an organization and spend minimal mental energy on what went well. As problem solvers, when there is no problem to solve there's nothing to be done, right?

One of the main signs that a job is done correctly is if it ends up becoming routine — it does the job well, no one complains about it, and it ends up fading into the background of more pressing issues.

The problem this presents is one of corporate culture. If only the most pressing problems are the ones that take up oxygen in the room, then more attention is paid to squeaky wheels. This might incentivize people to make their wheels squeaky in order to garner more attention, and that can spiral out of control pretty quickly.

To prevent such a situation, it is helpful to focus on the sort of things that are worthy of attention and work backward from there. Let me explain why Yembo built a relationship with a fine silver mint.

Startups have varied philosophies regarding their views on patents. This is a complex and nuanced matter, but Yembo has chosen to build a portfolio of patents for many reasons, mostly defensive.

The US government created the patent system because inventors were hoarding ideas. To foster innovation, they devised a program where inventors would document their inventions and describe them publicly in a way that someone skilled in the art could follow. In return for this disclosure, the government agreed to grant the patent holder with the right to exclude others from practicing the invention.

This makes patents valuable — the right to exclude others from practicing the invention can provide a competitive advantage. It can be bought, sold, or temporarily provided to other companies under a license. Done correctly, a patent portfolio can be a valuable asset to a company pioneering in a technical field.

The US government has three prerequisites all patent applications must meet to be eligible to be granted. The invention must be novel, useful, and non-obvious.[1] Let's dig into what each of those requirements mean.

The invention must be novel, in that if it has already been done before, it is already present in the collective body of knowledge and therefore adds no new value.

It must be useful, because the system exists for fostering innovation. Inventions that accomplish no practical purpose are not under the government's mandate to protect.

And it must be non-obvious, since obvious extensions of existing inventions do not genuinely expand humanity's collective understanding.

The patent examiner is a trained expert — a lawyer by training with a required technical background in the field of the invention. For AI patents, the patent examiners often have master's degrees in electrical engineering or computer science in addition to being licensed attorneys.

Their job is to decline the application unless the criteria laid out in US law are satisfied. The process can take one to two years and can easily cost $30,000 if a lot of back-and-forth correspondence is involved. However, my view is, broadly, that the pros of the patent system outweigh the cons despite the system's imperfections (I'm looking at you, patent trolls!).

At Yembo, we patent the key inventions that make our product work well, which has several benefits.

A patent provides an externally-validated testament to the novelty of the product. AI is so complicated that it can be hard to communicate to a layperson the difference between a product built from the ground up optimized for a particular business workflow versus one cobbled together from freely available off-the-shelf parts.

Since the patent allows the holder to exclude others from practicing the invention, this provides a competitive moat for our inventions.

There is a real and significant cost in terms of time, money, and energy required to get a patent, and the benefit to the engineering team can be indirect or theoretical.

Being granted a patent is a big win worthy of an appropriate celebration. But we weren't celebrating it.

I looked into what other companies do to incentivize patents. Some companies give cash bonuses when a patent is granted. Some gifted plaques with the title page laser-engraved into a brass plate.

Borrowing a cue from the United States Mint, we came up with the idea to mint a one-ounce pure silver coin for each patent, with the faces of each inventor on the front side of each coin.

Yembo's first patent coin, for US Patent No. 11,263,460

We wanted to devise a way to celebrate in a medium with high integrity that was not too pompous or awkward. But cool.

When I showed the idea to our legal counsel, he mentioned he hadn't seen anything similar in his 20 years as a patent attorney.

Cost is the most obvious factor when considering how to celebrate wins. But it doesn't have to cost much money for the approach to be effective. The coin cost about the same as the boring old brass plaque that so many companies offer to their inventors.

In the best of all worlds, all of Yembo's employees will have a coin minted in their honor one day.

Lesson Learned: Celebrating the wins can be just as important as fixing problems.

31

HIRE FOR ABILITY, NOT BY HISTORY

I had just finished dinner and opened up my laptop to finish off a few loose ends before the day was out. I was starting to get frustrated. We had the budget to hire another frontend engineer, but I was having trouble getting people to apply.

It felt like we had persevered for months to improve the product to get to the point where our client base was growing, and I suppose I had deluded myself into thinking that once the money arrived, there'd be a line of people out the door waiting to work at Yembo.

I was at the point where I had tapped out most of my immediate network — every good engineer I knew with the right background either already worked at Yembo or was unavailable for an irreconcilable reason.

I tried several channels, from volunteering to judge hackathon projects to the standard postings on AngelList and LinkedIn. This evening, I was working on a cold LinkedIn message that I could use to recruit candidates personally.

The plan, such as it was, was to read some blogs on how to write a cold email, put a passable first version together, and iterate based on the responses until I found something people responded to. Iteration again.

The problem, though, was that no one was responding. Worse than that, less than half of the recipients were even opening the message. It's hard to iterate on your messaging when the attempt fails before a word is read.

After asking every experienced recruiter and HR person I could find for feedback, I learned that my approach was off. Software job postings are a bit peculiar in that they can be quite black and white.

Often companies will list each language or technology the job will need and how many years of experience an ideal candidate would have in each area. Then an applicant can run down the list and see if they qualify.

Pretty cut and dried, right?

Sort of. Employers generally know that someone with 100% of the tech stack is rare, so they pad the posting with untrue requirements. This way, if someone who is 80% qualified applies, they can still be a good fit.

This behavior kicks off a vicious cycle where job seekers are incentivized to apply to jobs where they may only meet 60% or 70% of the listed qualifications, which encourages the employer to pad more, and things can get pretty nuts pretty fast.

I have seen a coding bootcamp graduate with 12 weeks of coding experience and a laundry list of 25 languages and software packages on their resume. Not likely.

The secret I've learned to hiring successfully is to hire someone who will perform well in the role you have in mind, not necessarily based on what they have done in the past. As investment disclaimers like to say, past performance does not guarantee future success.

Often we judge people's abilities to succeed by focusing too much on what they have accomplished before. We think a VP of Sales will be great because they've been a VP of Sales at another company. But under this line of reasoning, no one could ever become a VP of Sales because they would need to be one already to become one. So clearly, this approach is not the only way.

What ultimately worked was hiring not by posting a laundry list of technical requirements, but by hiring for the ability to do the job at hand. Hiring for ability is a much more difficult goal for a hiring manager, and part of the reason why so many settle for hiring for experience. Let's dig into how.

It is helpful to think of hiring for ability not as a compromise, but by taking a close look the perceived requirements for the job, and looking for creative alternatives. For example, if a candidate doesn't have experience in every software library desired but demonstrates an ability to learn on the job, perhaps that's a beneficial tradeoff to accept. After all, wouldn't you want to work with the kind of person who can absorb new information and advise the next time a new software library is being considered?

When hiring for ability, I like to ask myself a few questions to help shed some light on whether a person is likely to succeed in a role. I don't directly ask the candidate these questions, but by the end of the interview I like to have an understanding of these points:

- **What are this candidate's career aspirations?** With the pace of innovation and disruption today, career changes are fairly common. It is revealing to understand why the candidate is interested in making a career change. Would giving the job offer propel the candidate to where they ultimately want their career to go?

- **Why have they not achieved their goals in the new career path yet?** In the best case scenario, the individual is resourceful and motivated, but hasn't been given a strong opportunity yet. Or maybe they are just starting out. On the flip side, if the candidate is not making do with what they can, it can be a sign of lack of motivation.

- **Can the job provide something unique and valuable to the candidate?** Ideally, after a job offer is made, things work out for years to come. In this scenario, the candidate receives something of value that convinces them to stick it out. If you can clearly articulate that vision up front, it helps with alignment.

The ultimate hire I made for the position was Tiana Hayden, who you will meet next. Tiana joined Yembo as one of the first software engineers. She came from a nontraditional background to the software engineering profession, yet her past experience gave her acute abilities to build the right set of features and run a team effectively. She learned the ropes quickly, and went on to manage the engineering team for Yembo's overall moving product.

Lesson Learned: When hiring, remember that the people who have never done the job before may be the most eager to do it.

32

STARTUP FOLK: TIANA IN HER OWN WORDS

How did you first discover Yembo?

My journey to Yembo started before I considered myself a software engineer. I was midway through the coding bootcamp I was enrolled in when my dad cut out an article from the San Diego Union Tribune (a real newspaper, physically cut with scissors!) and put it on my bed.[1]

He frequently cut out articles he thought I would find interesting, and this was no exception. The article was about a budding AI startup in the area. It had a picture of Zach and Sid and a few of the first Yembo hires, and covered how Yembo was modernizing an unexpected industry with AI. Three things stood out to me in the article:

1. I thought the product was quite clever, made a lot of sense, and that it was a no-brainer to be successful.

2. I could sense the team's closeness and authenticity from the small black-and-white photo.
3. I was impressed that the founders who were young, not much older than I was, were able to create this team and product from an idea and a dream.

I finished reading and went back to my bootcamp studies. I had just left my full-time job overseas at Google and was back at home, living with my parents and figuring out what I wanted to do next with my life. Working at Google was amazing; I learned a lot about business and teamwork in a large organization. I was spoiled with free food, massages on campus, and generous pay — who in their right mind would want to leave? While the perks were fantastic, I missed my family, my hometown of San Diego, and I wasn't passionate about the actual work I was doing. I decided to see what else was out there, but I wasn't sure where that path would lead.

How did you decide to become a software engineer?

I tried many things while at home in this exploratory period, including a self-guided introductory Python programming class that I completed from various coffee shops around San Diego. Lo and behold, I ended up really liking the course. I love board games, and coding felt like a new game I was playing. As I played around with writing simple code, I enjoyed the process more and more. I felt part Nancy Drew solving a puzzle, part Rosetta Stone learning a language, and part carpenter building something new from scratch.

After doing some research, I discovered that there are coding bootcamps that teach hands-on, practical skills one would need to get hired as a software developer. I remember when I went and visited the bootcamp for the first time, I had an overwhelming feeling that this was the right next step for me, that I belonged here.

Fast forward a month later and I was enrolled. I loved my time at the bootcamp — it was just fun, it didn't feel like work. I started to dream about the problems I was solving in class. I was the first one there in the morning and among the last to leave. And even though I was one of only two women in the entire program, I felt like I fit in, that these were my people.

Tell me about your transition into a tech job.

I finished the course on time. But then came the hardest part, finding an employer to take a chance on a young bootcamp graduate with no real experience and without a full computer science degree. I watched some of the previous graduates get stuck taking interview after interview but not able to actually land a job.

After a few weeks of searching, I was able to leverage my network and previous work experience to land me my first development job as a frontend React Developer. I was so happy I cried when I found out I was hired. I felt like I somehow slipped in the door of an exclusive nightclub — I was an employed engineer! Although I wasn't on the typical guest list, I managed to get into the club and I wasn't leaving!

In this first job, I was able to build on the foundation of skills I learned at bootcamp. But after about a year, my growth was stagnating and I started thinking about moving on. Just at the point when I was thinking about applying to other companies, I got a message on LinkedIn from someone named Zach Rattner looking for frontend development talent.

He looked familiar, then I saw his title "CTO and Co-

Founder of Yembo." Oh right! Yembo, the budding AI startup from the Union Tribune article. I remembered him from the picture in the article! Now that I had the title of "software developer" on my LinkedIn profile, I frequently got messages from LinkedIn from recruiters and other CTOs. But because of that article, I decided to reply to Zach and we scheduled an informal chat to learn more about the position.

What was the transition to Yembo like?

After my introductory call with Zach, I knew I wanted to work for Yembo and for Zach specifically. You know when you talk to someone and just know they are operating at a higher level than most of us mere mortals? That's how I felt talking to Zach — I knew he was someone that was going places, and I wanted to go along for the ride.

And now that I have known Zach for many years, that initial impression has turned out to be 100% true. What makes Zach so powerful is his ability to get the big picture but also the technical details. He doesn't just know the business side, or just the engineering side, he understands the details in both areas. He knows enough about what each team is doing to speak their language, unblock as needed and to steer the ship in the right direction. He is the nerdy maestro of this software product symphony, and when we are all in tune — boy does it feel good! After that first phone call, I knew I wanted to be just like him.

I joined Yembo with the initial goal to learn everything I could from Zach technically and operationally. Being an overachiever, I found it challenging to not get everything right right away. I was still very new in my engineering career when I joined Yembo and I wanted so badly to contribute in all areas I could. But jumping into an existing code base as a new hire is hard — it took me a while to ramp up on each of the different codebases that Yembo used. I would sometimes feel overwhelmed when debugging something and go down rabbit holes with no successful outcome. In those moments, I questioned if I was "really an engineer" and able to do this type of work.

Did your prior work experience help you in your software engineering role?

When starting out and feeling overwhelmed by how much I did not know technically, it helped me to rely on my previous work experience. From my previous roles, I learned how to be organized, lead a project, work with customers, and be a good teammate — all skills that are transferable to any job. This gave me confidence in my competence, that I could figure something out if given enough time. I could come back to this confidence in moments when I was feeling unsure technically. This confidence also helped me when interviewing for the role — I could sell my previous experience as an asset, to make up for my lack of experience in advanced computer science concepts.

Early on in my Yembo career, I got to use specific experience from my previous role at Google to help Yembo scale. As Yembo was growing, so were the number of support requests sent to the engineering team (e.g. a customer needs help resetting their password, our internal team needing clarification about how a product works, or a user reporting a bug). Our engineering team was fielding these requests ad hoc over Slack. This works for fast communication when one engineer is getting a couple questions a day. But soon, the volume grew along with the engineering team and a few problems emerged:

1. It was unclear who should be responding to each question.
2. It was slowing down other engineering projects, as an engineer was frequently being disrupted throughout the day.
3. There was no tracking on the types of requests we were getting, so there was no way to monitor and optimize for success.

Should we have more training internally? Were bugs often being reported in a specific area over and over again? If we could answer these questions with data, we could make our product and customer experience better for everyone.

When I worked on the Global Customer Experience team at Google, I fielded similar support requests. Leveraging my experience there, I was able to put an official support process into place for Yembo. We started scheduling support hours for engineers, so it was clear who was expected to answer incoming questions and when. When an engineer wasn't scheduled to support, then she knew she could focus on her engineering work uninterrupted. We moved from a group chat open to everyone to one dedicated channel per request, so we could track the number of requests we were getting and minimize the noise. We also categorized each chat, so we could understand how to improve. I felt good about the efficiencies this initiative brought to the team.

What kind of challenges did you encounter as you grew in your technical role?

Since those early days, my engineering skills have improved immensely. I've written frontend and backend code, architected completely new processes from scratch, and even received my first patent for my engineering work on Smart Consult. As much as I've improved technically since I started at Yembo, I still fight those feelings that I'm "not a real engineer." I will make an architectural decision that in hindsight could have been better and think to myself, "if I was a real engineer, I wouldn't have made this mistake".

I have since learned that the name for this feeling is "impostor syndrome" and it's quite common among engineers. Still, these feelings surprised me because it's something I hadn't experienced before writing software.

Perhaps it comes about because I switched careers and came from a bootcamp background instead of a traditional computer science degree. Perhaps it's because there's so much to learn in writing and deploying software. Or perhaps because software languages and technologies move so fast, so it's impossible to know everything. Whatever the reason, impostor syndrome is something that I still struggle with to this day.

Thankfully, Zach and the team at Yembo have been there to reassure me and to promote my growth each step of the way. During my almost four years at Yembo, I progressed from writing frontend code that was scoped out for me, to writing frontend code I scoped out myself, to contributing to product decisions, completing backend projects, earning a patent, and now managing an entire codebase and multiple engineers.

If I was still working at a big company, it would have taken me ten years to get to where I am now. There are just so many opportunities when the company is growing fast and establishing itself, especially when you can work alongside smart, talented, and driven people. I have personally gained knowledge, grown and expanded right along with the company. Working at a startup has been the fastest way to understand how a business operates, and how to deliver impact at scale.

So I guess I have to say thanks Dad for cutting out that article for me all those years ago! I wouldn't want to be anywhere else than where I am now.

PART V

GROWING PEOPLE

33

EXERCISE: THE FRIEND AT THE DINNER TABLE TEST

W hile a larger company might require a certain amount of time before promoting an employee, at a startup one person's job can quickly balloon into four or five when the area they have been working on takes off.

In these cases, it's often more expedient for both the company and the employee to promote the individual contributor to a manager rather than try to find an outside manager to run the nascent team.

The time and energy taken to invest in the individual to train them to be an effective manager is often more economical than the risk of looking for outside management.

When it works out this way, everyone benefits — the employee enjoys an accelerated career trajectory, the new employees have the benefit of a manager who is technically capable in the area they are expected to work on, and the executives have the continuity of working with the same point of contact they were before the team scaled.

At Yembo, three engineers working on three different

product areas were in such a situation. One common question that kept coming up in my coaching conversations with them was if their expectations for their direct reports were reasonable. It is a valid question and one worth exploring a bit deeper.

Managers in this position are excellent individual contributors. They can often juggle competing priorities well, and they have an understanding of the product being worked on since its early days. So they don't need a lot of hand-holding on what needs to be done next in terms of implementation.

For strategy and direction, they still benefitted from my input, but in terms of running the business day-to-day, they were all quite capable.

Folks in this position generally have a long list of areas they'd like to be able to work on. But when a new person joins the team and the manager is new to management, a few challenges crop up. First off, the new hire doesn't have the benefit of context from day one.

They need to be told what to do enough to be effectively onboarded, but not so much that their job becomes routine and dull. When a new engineer's output wasn't what the manager expected, rather than jumping to blaming the engineer for underperforming, I noticed my managers were looking within.

Was too much being expected? Could anyone fill the expectations for the role?

Enter the Friend at the Dinner Table Test

This is where a test I like to call the Friend at the Dinner Table Test comes in. It's not perfect, but gives a good fingerin-the-wind check on whether expectations are reasonable.

Imagine you, a Shiny New Manager, face a tough conversation. You have a task that you want a team member to perform, but you know it's ambitious. You know it's not impossible, but you are not sure if the new employee can do the project. At the root of the issue, you're not sure if your expectations are aligned to reality or not.

Now imagine you go ahead and give the project to your employee and it doesn't go over well. That night, they are meeting with a friend at dinner and naturally, since you have massively irked them, they are griping about work. More specifically, they are griping about you and the unreasonable expectations you have dumped on them.

The test involves role playing — articulate what the employee would say in this situation and how the friend would respond. It can be helpful to run this exercise with another trusted peer and actually act out the situation.

Would the friend commiserate and say it's ridiculous?

Or would they suggest stopping being so pampered and stepping up to the challenge?

The exercise isn't perfect because naturally, people are unpredictable, and you can almost always contort the outcome to whatever you'd like. But the outcome itself isn't the point — the exercise of thinking through the situation from the employee's perspective and building empathy is.

The Friend at the Dinner Table Test has eased me out of shoveling far too much responsibility on someone else. On the flip side, it has led me to make a bet on people and make a few key promotions.

I was running through the test with an advisor when we were considering promoting an engineer to management and here's the line from the role-play that convinced me:

"Come on man, your manager is asking you to take ownership of a new product that you know customers want and are willing to pay for. He offered you resources, help with project planning, and mentorship along the way to step up to the task? And you are getting cold feet because you've never done this before? Do you know how many other people he could probably find that would yearn to get an opportunity like this?"

My Friend at the Dinner Table Test talked me into looking at things from a point of view I had not considered.

Context matters.

34

MICROMANAGEMENT: GET OFF
MY CASE

hen Apple started its streaming service, Apple did something they are notorious for doing. They micromanaged. The *New York Post* reported:[1]

Agents and producers can't stop griping about how "difficult" Apple is to deal with — citing a "lack of transparency," "lack of clarity" and "intrusive" executives, including CEO Cook.

One of the biggest complaints involves the many "notes" from Apple executives seeking family-friendly shows, sources said.

"Tim Cook is giving notes and getting involved," said a producer who has worked with Apple. One of the CEO's most repeated notes is "don't be so mean!," the source said.

"He's giving feedback," an agent said of Cook, adding that the CEO has been seen on the Vancouver set for "See," a futuristic drama about human kind without sight, and in LA for the production of a drama starring Reese Witherspoon and Jennifer Aniston.

Apple executives in general have been "very involved," this person said, adding that writers and directors prefer to work without corporate intrusions.

I'm thinking Hollywood is forgetting who's paying the bills.

Tim Cook's micromanagement style is probably why Apple is so successful in the first place. Without Cook's micromanagement of the supply chain, the iPad would probably cost $3,000.

But there is no doubt that micromanagement rubs a lot of people the wrong way. What exactly is micromanagement? It can loosely be defined as evaluating people or processes very closely. It's often perceived in a negative manner, which is probably a result of the fact that micromanagement seems to interfere with details better understood by other members of the team.

For instance, all those agents and producers in Hollywood think that they know better about details than Apple does. What they may not be considering, however, is that Apple wants the products released by its streaming service to reflect the culture of Apple.

Teams do generally feel that there is a strong negative correlation between the amount of micromanaging and the autonomy that employee has on a project. It's a fine line. Leaders have to differentiate between setting reasonable goals and tweaking each tiny detail of a process. President Jimmy Carter was famously accused of micromanaging because he put himself in charge of scheduling the White House tennis courts.

How can micromanagement be bad? The most obvious answer to that is it can have a very negative impact on employee morale. Employees feel that they are not being listened to and at some point, they just stop listening, or making suggestions for improvement, because they feel they won't be listened to. If there's a big problem going on in the company, employees might not be willing to spend their time working on it because they assume that their manager will take full credit for any success, or they simply don't care anymore.

This situation leads to employee disengagement, which winds up costing money. The performance of the employee is reduced because the manager, by micromanaging, has made the decision to remove any incentives for the employee to show effort and creativity. Micromanaging can lead to a lack of trust. The leader feels like the employee is not able to complete a process, and the employee gets frustrated by not being able to use his own ideas or autonomy to complete the process.

An element of cognitive dissonance can also be introduced by a leader who micromanages because it gives him an illusion that he is being effective, especially when things go well early, which is probably the point at which he is in there micromanaging.

This approach hurts the enterprise in the long term, so leaders should trust their employees to be creative and empower them to be bold. In sustainable organizations, the leader's success depends on their ability to surround themselves with a strong team that is positively reinforced to help the leader succeed.

On the other hand, as in the case of Tim Cook, sometimes it's just in the leader's nature to micromanage.

When is micromanaging good?

- When the strategy of the organization is taking a sharp turn (e.g., Apple starting a streaming service)
- A new project is starting
- There is a new division
- Employees are failing to execute an initiative

When these things happen a leader should be proactive, and yes he may have to micromanage by getting the boat back on course. Micromanagement might be one of the only ways to investigate the root problem in a dysfunctional process. It's very important however for employees to understand why the leader is getting involved personally. A leader can often diffuse any territorial issues by framing his management as offering support in everyone's pursuit of a common goal.

35

USING DEADLINES EFFECTIVELY

D eadlines. That's a word few people like to hear.

From grade school onward, society conditions us to work with deadlines. As a result, many of us grow to loathe them, and sometimes the authorities behind them too.

Turn in a perfect homework assignment after the deadline? Your teacher has a penalty waiting for you.

File your taxes late? The IRS has a penalty for that too.

Arrive at the airport five minutes after the plane takes off? Good luck.

Deadlines are often misunderstood. In a startup, there is ambient pressure to deliver now. "What's the deadline?" is often a foolish question to ask, since the answer always seems to be "as soon as possible."

Sam Altman, CEO and Co-Founder of OpenAI, puts it succinctly:

"Move faster. Slowness anywhere justifies slowness everywhere."[1]

What's going on here? Are all startups run by impatient

Type A dictatorial types? Perhaps some are, but that's not the crux of the matter.

Startups are by their nature disruptive. Pick one of your favorite startups, because we're going to use it as a case study. Now think about how that startup's industry worked before the startup came along.

Perhaps things weren't ideal, but things worked. Need a ride to the airport before Uber? It was clunky, but a cab would get you there. Need to send a note to someone before America Online? The US Postal Service would gladly do the job.

All startups face inherent inertia — that is, resistance to change. There is already a status quo that is working well for incumbents. These incumbents have power (because they're incumbents) and are generally resistant to change, because the status quo is working for them. So the startup's mission is to re-educate and evangelize change until the incumbents adapt or are unseated.

These changes take time. We still have thought leaders talking about "digital transformation" decades after the advent of the Internet.

Unfortunately, time is often not on the startup's side. Venture-backed startups are generally expected to hit their next milestone and raise their next investment round every two years or so which is not a lot of time when it comes to reforming markets.[2] Personnel and business infrastructure are recurring expenses, so there is a real monetary cost to every second of existence (not that I've ever calculated ours at Yembo, of course).

This sense of urgency trickles down into everything a healthy startup does — waiting a day to get back to a client request delays their expansion. Letting a contractor ignore a deadline risks missing a marketing event. Looking into a security alert tomorrow risks getting hacked today.

How does this all relate to deadlines? There are a few approaches I've found to work when setting deadlines in a startup context:

- **Avoid setting deadlines when you can**. If a task takes two minutes or less to do, just do it when it comes up. This is much more effective than taking down a note and having someone do it later.
- **Have your deadlines be real**. If you treat deadlines as suggestions, it confuses rather than motivates. Resist the urge to throw out arbitrary deadlines — put in the effort to plan a project, bringing in relevant stakeholders and factoring their input into the plan. Track progress along the way so if things veer off track you are aware as soon as it happens, not later when the deadline is missed. Devise a Plan B when the deadline is approaching and you are not confident you can hit the deadline. Do retrospectives after deadlines to identify where workflows could be improved.
- **Hold yourself to deadlines and encourage others to as well.** Remember that most people have learned to live with deadlines but not to love them. You can help break that mold as a leader by being willing to hold your deliverables to the same level of rigor around timelines as you hold your team. For example, if you agree to recruit a new employee to help an existing team, be willing to share your timeline and intermediate progress

along the way to keep them in the loop. Exhibit the discipline you want others to follow.

Lesson Learned: Great leaders have strategic patience. They are committed for the long term to see their vision through, but they do not allow tactical steps along the way to bloat with unnecessary delays.

36

SHOULD I STAY?

P eople have different reasons for joining a startup.

One evening, I was researching employee retention at startups, and I found some interesting data on how long employees tend to stay at companies. There's about an 80% probability that someone is still at a job after one year.[1] Through voluntary termination or otherwise, the remaining 20% of the cohort are no longer employed at the same company within one year of starting. The retention probability reduces to about 60% after two years. And after three years, the probability drops below 50%.

The statistic followed a negative exponential distribution, which seemed a bit suspect. Think of all the famous startups whose products we use often — Airbnb, Dropbox, Snapchat — could it be true that most employees turned over within three years? How does the business operate? Wouldn't they be stuck in training and onboarding constantly?

I was determined to figure out why, so I asked around. And from my findings, the main reason is that when people don't feel challenged anymore, they leave. Great people push themselves to do better so they can master their craft. By fostering an environment where great people can do the best work of their careers, the company can accomplish things that have never been done before. Accordingly, we try to challenge our employees.

There are multiple paths that lead individuals to join a startup. Some people want to take a risk and bet on themselves, while others grow tired of bureaucracies at larger companies and want to be more pragmatic.

While it's ok to have various reasons for a candidate being interested in the startup, it is helpful to make sure they are in it for the right reasons.

What makes someone initially interested in a company might not be the thing that convinces them to stay.

Startups tend to place a lot of focus on recruiting, but retention is equally important. Fortunately, the skillset required to be good at one is helpful to the other.

With recruiting, it is helpful to know what qualities an ideal candidate has and filter candidates based on an assessment of the likelihood of excelling in the role. Find out what the candidate is most interested in achieving in their career. If the position provides that, sell it hard. Explain practically why it would be a great fit.

The secret to being convincing is to have a clear plan and tell the truth about how the candidate can achieve their goals in the role.

After joining, retention comes down to a similar problem. Just as in recruiting, the search problem is to find the right candidate for the role in mind. The challenge is to align the company's future needs with the employee's ambitions.

If you can find an area the company needs to fill that the employee is interested in working in, then you are set. In other words, the value proposition for each employee as to why they work at the company should be just as crisp three or four years in as it was on day one.

As a leader, you are responsible for figuring this out for your employees.

At Yembo, we have been fortunate to have multiple key employees who have been there for three or more years, which is exactly how we like it. They're nice people. What's not to like?

When I look at the employees who have stayed beyond three years, I notice a trend. These folks had significantly different day-to-day lives than they did when they joined. So they were still changing jobs within the three years; it's just that we were able to find another job for them at the same company.

For example, we've had a frontend developer become a lead product designer, an individual contributor become a product lead, and a customer success manager become a department head.

The reasoning behind this is clear. People join startups to grow, and if their growth trajectory tapers off, over time they run the risk of leaving. It is much more efficient to continue this growth within the same company, provided the opportunity exists.

There is a high context switching cost of changing jobs — losing the context of how things work, the camaraderie and working relationships, and the uncertainties that come with navigating new corporate politics.

To the extent it can be done, fostering long-term relationships and building a company where people want to stay makes for a much more effective workflow.

37

OR SHOULD I GO?

It was the winter of 2020, and I was flying back to San Diego after a high-profile customer visit. We had two frontend engineers due to join the company on the following Monday.

I had just landed in San Diego and taken my phone out of airplane mode when I received an email from one of the engineers due to join the following week. Just by looking at the subject line, I knew what it meant — he wasn't going to be joining:

Availability

████████████ ████████████████████   Thu, Jan 16, 2020, 9:27 AM
to me

Hey Zach,

Do you have some availability today to chat?

My gut feeling turned out to be right.

He found another job with a shorter commute and reneged on the offer.

Fortunately, I hadn't even taken down the job posting yet. Still on the tarmac, I was scrolling through messages. I saw a note from a qualified candidate — she had a computer science degree with a strong GPA and was interested enough in our company to reach out even though she didn't have any prior relationships with anyone at the company:

[yembo-careers] Full-Stack Web Product Developer (React)

 Noel Kennebeck   ✉ Thu, Jan 16, 2020, 5:51AM
to careers

Hi! I am applying for the Full-Stack Web Product Developer position at Yembo.

I've attached my resume, and my earliest start date would be February 17th.

Let me know if you need anything else from me, thank you!
Noel

I looked over her resume and was impressed. I forwarded the resume to my co-founder with my usual thorough summary of the situation:

 Zach Rattner   ✉ Thu, Jan 16, 2020, 7:24AM
to Siddharth

Pretty good background.

Noel interviewed well — we gave her a take-home assignment to build a web page with an accelerometer-tracking algorithm that detects when the phone is swung like a ping-pong paddle.

Noel's four years of NCAA Division 1 volleyball helped —

her swing detection algorithm worked quite well. Most candidates only handled the strength of the acceleration, but Noel's algorithm considered the direction of the swing as well.

The interview process went smoothly, and the team was impressed with her background. During deliberations after the interview, the one thing that stood out as strange to us was why she applied. She's from Seattle, went to school in upstate New York, lived in Boston, and wanted to move to San Diego and join a company most people have never heard of. Something didn't add up. My co-founder was convinced she'd move away when the allure wore off within a year or two.

But she was qualified, so I proceeded with an offer.

Ultimately my co-founder was right — Noel did move out of San Diego a couple of years later. That said, Covid had transformed Yembo into a fully remote company by then, so it wasn't the end of her time at Yembo. She climbed the ranks quickly and her move to Seattle coincided with a promotion to Software Engineering Manager.

We started working together because we were a tech company with an interesting use case and a modern tech stack. It also helped that we were located in a city she was interested in moving to.

While the allure of San Diego was sufficient to get her in the door, we had to adapt to make an environment where she would be interested in staying. Noel may have been at the same company for three years but hasn't had the same job for three years.

The lesson I learned from working with Noel is that the reason that someone might want to join a company isn't necessarily the reason that they will want to stay.

38

STARTUP FOLK: NOEL IN HER OWN WORDS

How did you transition to Yembo?

My first job after I graduated from college was at a large company; in that role I benefited from the big-company structure, but soon realized that I wasn't offered the flexibility to continue learning.

Working on a single product and in a technical silo made it difficult to explore new opportunities outside of my assigned work, and after about a year it became clear that my role would not offer the learning that I desired.

I realized that, to continue growing, I would need to find a new role at a new company — preferably a startup with great growth opportunities.

At the time, I had some friends that worked at startups and my partner was working at a startup incubator. They were all enjoying their jobs and their companies had multi-year runways that gave them confidence in their job security — this told me that the risk profile of joining a startup was much lower than I had thought it to be.

I was eager to try something different after my first role and excited to escape the cold after years in the Northeast. In my spare time I browsed San Diego startup job boards, and indiscriminately applied to open roles in the interest of better understanding the landscape.

As a recent grad with a thin resume I had a long and difficult job search process, but I was setting my sights high because I didn't want to settle for another entry-level software engineering role.

The search lasted several months and consisted of many multiple-hour coding interviews that frankly went horribly — I was expected to have memorized algorithms and all the intricacies of multiple programming languages; most processes disregarded the problem-solving skills and ability to learn quickly that I knew made me a great software engineer. After a few disheartening interviews I thought I was going to have to settle for a subpar company and role, and then (as though by magic, or AI) I found Yembo.

What was interviewing at Yembo like?

When I interviewed at Yembo, I was asked questions such as "what's interesting to you?" or "what do you like?" or "what are you looking for?". Those questions surprised me because I wasn't hearing them in other job interviews.

That experience wasn't typical, but neither is working here. As the company has grown I've been able to grow with it, and I've been able to build a unique career trajectory that aligns my interests with the company's goals.

How would you describe your responsibilities at Yembo?

Yembo suits my personality because my job is constantly changing, which means I am constantly learning. Our company and my role are often amorphous, but I'm well-suited to that dynamic. When my day-to-day gets repetitive and I am no longer being challenged, I can create a clear and steady path for my work and then tackle one of the many other new challenges that are always available to us. This helps keep me engaged in my work.

I often feel that I perform best when there are very clear expectations, but as I've progressed further into my career, I've learned that I need to create my own expectations. Clear goals are inherent to software engineering, especially at the entry-level: "Here's a ticket to complete. Did I do it right? Did I do it quickly?".

These questions come with the territory in engineering, but I'm also a little bit more on my toes here because I am also required to have strong interpersonal skills. I can't just be a lone programmer sitting off by myself — nor do I want to be.

I'm expected to build software to achieve business goals, which requires working with the team and different stakeholders. I have a great deal of agency in decision-making — often, I play a key role in defining what features we ship.

What was transitioning into management like?

One person can only do so much, and building large-scale software requires working with a team. As I gained confidence and competence as an individual contributor, managing teams was a clear next step. I began by managing remote teammates in Ukraine, then folks in the US.

I feel as though I have a knack for managing teams, leading a product and being responsible for the work happening. It's problem-solving with a different set of variables; instead of code, I use words and planning to achieve my desired outcome. This has been a new and exciting challenge in my career.

People like me don't want to be doing the exact same thing every day.

When a company is small, there are few clearly defined roles and there's always more work than people. For me, this is a great challenge. Larger companies may have more structured opportunities, but in general I've been very happy working in a startup environment where I can build my own path.

Because there is always too much to do and not enough people to do it, there is often flexibility in who tackles what. You can gravitate to the kind of work you find yourself most interested in, and that's ok. As a team, you'll find ways to take care of the rest.

By the time I arrived at Yembo, I was mentally ready for a workplace characterized by growth and change. I like the track I'm on, and I have the opportunity to be responsible for a team and a product.

It's exciting to be at a company with no set career trajectory, because that means I get to define it myself.

39

ON THE PAYROLL

M uch has been written about compensation negotiations. To many, it feels like a game. My experience has been that if you treat compensation like a game, others will too. A friend told me he received a 40% salary increase by submitting his resignation and waiting for the counteroffer. His employer played games with compensation. Now that his story is out, it encourages others to submit resignation letters just to see what happens.

The situation gets out of hand quickly.

Here's how it works: the hiring manager posts a job opening, and candidates start applying.

Hiring budgets have historically been fairly opaque, but needlessly so — who posts a job without budgeting first? Many states are passing laws to make this more transparent, which may help reduce unnecessary gamesmanship in recruiting.

Recruiters have traditionally asked the candidate to provide their current salary or to proffer their salary requirements. In the past, a recruiter has even required me to upload my most recent pay stub to prove I wasn't inflating the number. This serves no practical purpose other than to anchor the candidate lower even if the budget for the position is higher.

While this behavior can save money for the employer in the short term, it encourages distrust. The employer is using their asymmetric information advantage to take advantage of candidates, and as a result, the candidates feel justified in playing games to counter.

This is not setting the stage for a long-term healthy relationship.

If, on the other hand, the compensation is clearly laid out in the job posting and the criteria is listed, everyone is aligned. The employer can take the position that they want to compensate each employee as much as they possibly can but they have a budget to work with. Then everyone is incentivized to do great work and build products that make customers happy, and everyone wins.

This also removes the incentive for employees to submit resignation letters as a tactic to get pay increases. If the pay for the role is shared in advance, and the employer takes steps to proactively increase compensation through salary increases, equity grants, and/or bonuses before the employee asks, then several key benefits are provided for both parties:

- The employee is fairly compensated.
- The employee doesn't need to "fight" for their compensation, meaning the manager can focus time on building products versus handling high stakes negotiations.

- If someone does request a counteroffer, it becomes a simple conversation because they are already being paid at top of the budget. The 40% increase scenario can't happen because that slack was already given up front. Rather than the employee advocating for themselves and the employer batting them down, the employer can say, "I also want you to be able to make that. We have a line of sight into making that happen. Let's achieve X/Y/Z goals for the company; then we'll be in a position to have the cash flow to make that happen."
- The employer can forecast their spend with more certainty, since there is no risk that the budget will increase 40% overnight based on factors outside of their control.
- Everyone trusts each other more and can have a productive relationship.

There is a line in the 1959 play *A Raisin in the Sun*, "Money is life."[1] And there is certainly some truth to this statement.

Lesson Learned: If you treat compensation like a game, others will too. Best not to.

Not that I've calculated this, but if you assume an average person needs 2,000 calories per day to live, and average daily expenditure on food is about $20, then a calorie is worth about a penny. You are expending calories at work, and you're trying to bring home excess calories in the form of money.

Money is a serious business, which is why people get emotional about it.

So if you are upfront and respectful with your current and potential employees about money, you can mute emotional responses.

40

LETTING GO TO LET OTHERS FLOURISH

I wasn't sure whether to feel proud or anxious.

We were amassing some technically amazing parts of our product, but I felt my grasp and understanding of them was slowly slipping away.

We had just launched Smart Consult, our live AI video chat product that allows movers to discuss with the customer while the AI is identifying and counting items in the room.[1]

In our testing, we saw it could simplify the walkthrough process by a factor of three, meaning sales agents could carry on three times as many survey appointments in a day if they used the tool. But as we started to roll things out, there was a laundry list of smaller feature requests that clients brought up.

Some were deemed more important than others. Our team prioritized them in order of the number of surveys they would unlock and rolled straight from working on the initial product launch to the incremental requests that were coming in from clients.

The requests seemed to be coming in from all over the place, which in hindsight, is a good sign that customers are working to adopt. We had requests to support more devices and browsers, and add background blurring (this was 2020 — many moving companies had staff working from home, and they didn't want clients to see their old Bee Gees posters). It was busy, but the worst thing you can hear after launching a new product is silence.

There was one feature request that seemed simple on the surface but turned out to be quite difficult to implement. A team mentioned that their company's built-in microphones were low quality, and as a result their head of sales purchased Bluetooth headsets for the team.

But our product Smart Consult had a limitation where, for simplicity during development, the product selected the first microphone available when preparing to join the video call. It didn't seem like a complicated change, but there was some urgency behind it because the team didn't want to adopt the product unless they could put their best foot forward to the customer.

I thought it would be a good project for one of the newer engineers on the team, so I wrote up the project description in our project management tool and assigned the task to him. I let him know if he ran into any issues I'd be available to discuss, and I moved on to work on something else.

When he submitted the code back, it was great. He had added a subtle, unobtrusive dropdown menu that let the user select which camera and microphone in the event there were multiple. If there was only one, the product accepted the defaults and had the same seamless experience.

When I reviewed the way he implemented the logic to enumerate the devices and display the dropdown list, there were a few parts I didn't completely understand. It was clear to me this was not as simple a task as it had seemed, yet the implementation worked beautifully.

Modern devices often have multiple cameras and microphones; some are better than others. For example, the consumer would want to join the call with the camera facing them, but the mover would want the ability to have the camera face the room so they could document the items present.

It took some effort to distinguish between which cameras face which way, what microphone to use when there are multiple, and presenting it in a way that was clear so the default works for the majority of users.

On one hand, I was thrilled that the engineer could take on the new task and do it well.

But on the other hand, I was nervous that I was slowly losing an understanding of my own codebase.

If I didn't understand what was in the codebase, how could I be expected to manage timelines and customer expectations? What would happen if that engineer took a vacation, or worse, quit?

As the complexity of the product grew, so did my anxieties that one day I would slowly morph into Bill Lumbergh from *Office Space*, reduced to announcing "Remember, next Friday Is Hawaiian Shirt Day!"

With the benefit of hindsight, we have the luxury of dispassionately observing situations and considering various scenarios. If we give in to an oblique fear, things can quickly devolve.

As CTO, I am responsible for the company's general technology solutions. This means I split my time across all areas of the tech stack — frontend, backend, infrastructure, and design.

If I feel I must be the alpha engineer on the team in each of these areas, it then sets a low bar for everyone else on the team. If I can only expect to spend a handful of hours a week on any one area, then it stands to reason that I would not be able to put in the time to genuinely master that craft.

On the other hand, if I give in and let others take over, the very real concern that I would lose the ability to manage the project cannot be ignored. What happens if a support ticket comes in while the anchor engineer who wrote the feature is on vacation? It would be embarrassing if I couldn't answer questions about my own company's product.

It's relatively simple to manage someone doing similar tasks as yourself. But to manage someone who can do things you cannot do yourself, you need to learn to ask good questions. That requires venturing to learn enough about how their world works to grasp the constraints they are working under.

Ultimately, we solved the problem with a bit of knowledge sharing. We used our internal knowledge base Yembuddy, where engineers could post notes, diagrams, and troubleshooting tips on the areas of the product they built.

The goal was not to have any one person with an equal understanding of the entire codebase, but rather to allow any engineer to ramp up on that area if they needed it. This was key because requiring anyone to understand everything would restrict the sophistication we could build into our products.

This approach allowed the engineers to feel free to pursue complex tasks if they needed to, and alleviated the burden on everyone else to feel compelled to understand everything as the product's feature set grew.

As a manager, you set the team's pace and attitude. The team dynamics inherit from the tone you set as the leader.

Confidence begets confidence and anxiety begets anxiety. But it is crucial to project confidence properly. Confidence can be empowering when grounded in sound reasoning and catastrophic if rooted in fantasies.

A clear-sighted manager can project confidence because they have learned to trust their own problem-solving skills and their team's abilities.

It's relatively simple for someone to solve a problem that they've already done before.

But to accomplish something new, you must learn to leverage other people's expertise.

41

EMPOWERING OTHERS

One of the benefits often overlooked by a perennial job hopper in search of a larger paycheck is the compounding effect of long-term relationships over time. There is only so much time over the course of one or two years to be productive, and if after ten years in the workforce each professional relationship is only one year deep, there's a limit to how effective the network can become.

In my career, some of my most valuable relationships have been over long periods. I worked alongside Sid for five years before starting Yembo with him. Now that we've known each other more than 10 years, we can practically complete each other's thoughts and sentences.

It's much easier to find alignment, disagree healthily, and work productively with someone you know very well. Some of our advisors and investors I have similarly known and collaborated with for over 10 years.

As an employee, when your employer is willing to take a long-term view, opportunities can be justified that are difficult otherwise. Certain decisions make economic sense with a long time horizon that are not justifiable in a shorter time period.

For example, imagine you work in human resources at an established company. Your manager asks you to allocate the company's budget for employee training. If the company's median tenure is 18 months, then anything more than short-term vocational training will be difficult to justify.

If, on the other hand, the company can reliably count on key employees staying around for five to 10 years, a whole new range of options may make sense. Remember that nothing else has changed across these two scenarios except for the median tenure — the repercussions are significant.

So how does a company gear itself for long-term, highly productive, engaged employees? Simply put, the organization must empower others. As a manager, you should aim to have your employees do things they have never done before in their careers. By continually being sharpened, challenged, and mastering new crafts, there's simply no time for boredom to sink in.

An effective manager should aim for harmony in a team, not homogeneity. Everyone can be doing different things, but the result needs to come together and achieve business goals. Expectations for the team should be personalized, allowing each employee to take advantage of their unique strengths and talents.

To do this well, the manager must know the employee's strengths and manage their weaknesses. A star contributor engineer may perform exceptionally well in product development but struggle when presenting to clients.

An adept management strategy will put the employee in situations approximately 10% beyond their abilities — enough to stretch but not too much to break.

The expectations will differ according to the area and the employee's abilities. In the star coder example, it may take a new tech stack or product area to stretch their technical skills, but basic public speaking training may be sufficient to challenge their presentation skills.

Having open-ended conversations around career goals can help facilitate these conversations. The employee must understand the manager has the employee's best interests in mind and wants to provide a fertile environment for growth and to accomplish new things. A productive outcome should not be expected if the mindset is of interrogation and exposing weaknesses.

Here are some questions I have found helpful to use in one-on-one conversations in getting to the heart of what makes an employee tick and what they want to accomplish in their careers:

"What are some things you've accomplished at work in the last two years that you are particularly proud of?"

This can help a conversation get going because it focuses on something specific and doesn't require much imagination to plan out the future. If you're not sure why the employee is proud of those things, ask them why.

"Imagine it's two years from now and you are out at dinner raving to your friends about how awesome your job is. What are some things you could have accomplished that would have led you to do this?"

Now we bring the imagination aspect in, but rather than leaving it too open-ended, we've painted a specific picture and asked the employee to fill in the blanks. This sort of open-ended thinking with the wheels greased can help the employee articulate their thoughts because you're making them picture themselves in a new situation and describe the scene to you.

"Here are some projects we have coming up on the horizon. Do you have a preference for which one you would like to take on?"

When there are multiple projects to be done, it can be quite revealing to solicit which areas people would like to work on versus deciding and assigning work. This also provides an environment to talk hypothetically about what each path would look like, which again helps make an abstract concept of where someone wants to go in their career more concrete.

"What skills would you like to exercise more often?"

Many employees struggle to articulate what role they want to grow into, and some flexibility can be beneficial. By focusing more on particular skills, workflows, and situations the employee would like to spend more time doing, a career path can be charted versus focusing on a particular lofty goal such as "I want *your* job, Zach."

After we closed our Series A at Yembo, we hired new engineers and started working on new products alongside the existing platform. We had several budding new leaders on the engineering team who had previously worked alongside me as an individual contributor, and had since grown to take on engineering leadership responsibilities in various product areas.

I shared a memo in our Slack channel to memorialize

some observations and lessons learned from the products I was personally responsible for shipping. The transparency helped the newer crop of engineering leaders to understand what aspects of the workflow were intentionally designed for efficiency and some things to look out for to ensure things are moving smoothly.

Here is the memo below, lightly edited to clarify internal jargon:

———————————————————————————

Here are some timelines on our recent products from planning meeting to production ship date (calendar days, includes weekends and holidays):

1. Local Estimates: 140 days

2. Interstate Estimates: 91 days

3. Smart Consult: 85 days (This one moved at legendary speed)

4. Telephony and Email Sync: 125 days

I wanted to share some lessons I've learned from these projects, especially for the folks working on newer products since we don't have a formal release cadence or customer base set up there yet:

• When planning the product, aim to find a viable feature set that can get in the customer's hands relatively quickly. This allows you to get feedback and iterate your way to maturity. Around 4-6 months maximum is ideal for software products (AI takes longer, but UI can fill AI gaps.) Much longer and you can lose sight of what the goal is.

• Know your strengths and make sure you have the right expertise on the team. For example, we didn't try to build our own video chat infrastructure with Smart

Consult [our live video chat + AI analysis product]. You can use a third-party service to get started faster and take it in-house after you ship. Sometimes these third-party services can be temporary — they can let you ship faster and you can re-evaluate after you launch. Time to market is key, and often the feedback you get from real customers by shipping sooner is worth the trade-off of not entirely building everything in-house.

• Incorporate design early. When you skip this step, you run into unexpected edge cases and have to figure out high level requirements as you're implementing. Walking through workflows in a Figma as a team before breaking dirt is gold.

• Leverage remote teams to make progress 24 hours a day. We strategically picked India and Ukraine because of the time zone difference — they work when you're sleeping! Get a remote buddy and hand off tasks before you leave for the day, wake up and have progress made. Estimates would have taken about three months longer if we didn't have this. Smart Consult might never have happened.

• Eat your proverbial dog food — most products we've done had a team of 5 to 10 engineers working on it. That's plenty of folks to test various features and share feedback. Test the area you didn't personally work on. For example, with our telephony features, we took turns calling each other daily. By the time the product launched, we already had multiple people use the product like a customer would and ironed out quite a number of kinks.

• Stay humble — it's hard to take critical UI feedback, but the truth is most first versions of anything need work. People give feedback because they care and want to improve the product; it's not an indictment on the implementer's ingenuity or creativity. Fortunately, we have an amazing team who is consistently open to feedback but not shy to debate until everyone's on the same page.

Looking back at the two years since I posted this memo, the top engineers who are leading products are still following these guidelines and shipping great features often.

The written word lives longer than a conversation, and can be a great source of continued motivation and inspiration.

42

NEWS TRAVELS FAST

G ood news tends to travel fast. The big deal that's closed, the investor that's in, the feature that customers love. There's a reason sales teams like to keep gongs around — they build camaraderie and celebrate wins together. When you're winning you want everyone to know. And there's nothing wrong with this in and of itself.

But, there are setbacks, promising opportunities that didn't work out, rejection, criticism. Bad news lacks curb appeal, and no one likes to share it. So as a result, many people don't.

If the deal doesn't come through, people tend to avoid discussing it. You can't prevent bad news from happening, but you can manage the fallout of what happens next. If you can overcome the discomfort of having to be the one to share bad news, you will be able to motivate others and inform them of the next steps.

Good news is easy to share because there aren't burdensome repercussions to deal with. But with bad news, there often are. When delivering bad news, consider it your responsibility to alleviate some of those repercussions to the recipient. This conveys that you have had time to think through the repercussions and gives authority to your words.

If you're talking about a promising opportunity constantly and then stop, rumors get started. Rumors are dangerous because someone else is controlling the narrative. This affects progress in many insidious ways. They can demotivate, undermine trust in the company's trajectory, and cause cliques.

Speak up early

The longer the gap between the event occurring and the news being disseminated, the more opportunities for leaks and rumors to spread. It's generally advisable to share as soon as you reasonably can.

Say it's bad

If you sugarcoat bad news, you erode credibility. People are generally smart and see through the veneer to what's really happening. My favorite line to break the ice? "I've got some bad news to share."

Get to the point

Explain what happened. Condense the bad news down to one sentence and deliver it up front. This gets the cat out of the bag and lets people process what it means. This can be a bombshell, so people might take a minute to process it. If you keep talking after dropping the news, people might miss it, so it's helpful to pause briefly after this part.

Explain the narrative

If there is a relevant context that puts the news in perspective, share that. If you've already prepared the next steps, share that too. If the news directly affects the person you are sharing with, think through the top questions they will probably ask and come prepared to share that here.

Tell who knows

Don't make it ambiguous who knows the news. If you are expecting something to be kept confidential indefinitely, explain that. If you want to break the news to someone else but haven't had the chance to yet, bring that up.

Here's an example bringing them all together:

Hey Sue, unfortunately I have some bad news to share with you. Jane will be leaving the company at the end of the month. She wanted to break the news to her direct reports but she asked if I could inform the other department heads.

She's been working with a friend on a startup idea over the weekends, and they have an idea they feel is going to be worthwhile.

While it's not the news I wanted to hear, I do want to wish her the best and support her. She has already put together a succession plan and I should be able to have it reviewed by HR by the end of the week. We're going to make an announcement at our next all hands meeting but I wanted to give you a heads up.

Yembo opened a Ukraine team in 2018. Some of the best frontend web engineers I have worked with are on that team. In the December 2021 performance review cycle, we promoted several software engineers to management positions and gave them teams composed of both US-based engineers and engineers in Ukraine.

The night Russia invaded in February 2022, I slept maybe 45 minutes in total. I was checking Telegram, Twitter, New York Times, and anything else I could find to get updates from. I sent some Slacks to the team to see if they were safe, but didn't get a response until the morning. By the time the work day started, I still had no clear answers.

Even though nothing was resolved, I didn't want the team to read the news and be confused about whether the team was safe and what Yembo was doing. So I called an emergency meeting with all the managers first thing in the morning, and then posted a message in our general Slack channel for everyone to see:

February 24, 2022 • 10:25 a.m. PST

We are closely monitoring the situation in Ukraine, which unfortunately has deteriorated in the last 24 hours. I am in contact with Andriy, our lead there, and his latest report as of 10am PST today was that the team is safe. One member, Dmytro, is in the reserve and got called into duty, but the other members are home. They are based out of Zhytomyr, which is about 150km due west of Kyiv. I have asked him to provide me with daily updates if he can, provided he can do so safely and without risk to himself or his family.

Our primary responsibility is to do what we can to make sure the team is taken care of there. In my last two meetings with Andriy, we discussed assisting with relocating those who wanted to leave, but their preference was to remain. We have offered a no-questions-asked time off policy to let folks take the time to stock up on supplies and take care of their families.

The engineering team met this morning to discuss each ongoing project and how they may be affected. Most projects are proceeding as planned:

• Mariner: Room Review redesign is still set to launch March 9.

• Mariner: Tiana is able to pick up the Onsite work as needed. We'll proceed as planned but may end up with delays.

• Kepler: Underwriting insured is in a stable state, future work is anyway pending customer feedback.

• Kepler: Backend is in good shape, with the India and Mexico teams handling most of the work there.

• Kepler: Annotation work may slip into Q2 as Kyle needs to fill in for Dmytro, but we can move the PDF report feature forward with the pool of candidates who have applied on Upwork.

I made a dedicated Slack channel for updates from the Ukraine team and related efforts. I've added everyone who I know works with the Ukraine team to the channel. If anyone else would like to be added, feel free to shoot me a DM and I can add you to #ukraine-updates.

We are hoping and praying the situation de-escalates soon. If anyone has any questions, please feel free to reach out to me — my Slack is always open.

No one enjoys giving bad news, but done professionally, the effects can be mitigated, and frustrations can be motivated in productive directions.

PART VI

LOOKING FORWARD

"Anything you want, it can be done"

Fog (Again) • Radiohead • COM LAG (2plus2is5) EP

43

MANAGING UNCERTAINTY

When I was weighing the decision to pursue the startup route, I got the sense from some of my friends that they viewed startups as a crapshoot. Toss the dice, see what comes out. The successful ones got lucky, the unsuccessful ones had a bad idea in the first place. The household names — Mark Zuckerberg, Bill Gates, Elon Musk, Steve Jobs — these guys all were lucky, but Friendster, MySpace, and Pets.com were simply the wrong horse to bet on.

While there is certainly an element of timing and things that need to go right outside of a founder's control for a startup to work out, there is a major problem with this oversimplification. The fundamental flaw lies in assuming there is one singular decision to make that determines a startup's success. In reality, a startup's trajectory is determined by many decisions made over a long period.

Some of the most pivotal moments in a startup's development are initiated by events outside a founder's immediate control:

- An important customer expressing interest in a partnership
- A channel partner expressing interest in a distribution deal
- A key hire coming on the market
- A major vendor experiences a data breach
- A strategic investor expressing interest in doing a deal
- The macroeconomic climate changing significantly, changing risk appetite

So while it's helpful to have goals and timelines the team can be working towards, the best founders I have worked with are adept at mitigating the risk that comes with uncertainty. In lieu of a crystal ball, below are a few tools that can be used to manage uncertain futures:

Get feedback on plans

One of the most painful situations for a founder is when the first version of the product is finally ready, and customers aren't using it. It's easy to get tunnel vision and continue building features without validating that they are the ones that will solve customers' problems.

To mitigate this situation, it's helpful to clearly articulate what you plan to do, and get feedback on that plan. For software projects, this can mean presenting wireframes, sketches, or mockups of the software before it's designed. For demo days and trade shows, this can mean drawing a floor plan of the booth layout and running through the pitch in a dry run before printing all the materials. There is a significant time (and currency) cost to executing, so it's helpful to put a crisp plan together and get feedback on that before investing in doing the project.

Budget for the unexpected

If the startup is an organism, your capital is oxygen, and you should not run out of it. This means doing the basics — balance the books, track spending, forecast costs versus revenues and update the model regularly in the early days when many parts are in flux at once. If you have multiple decision makers, you can give operating budgets to others on the team so they can work within your planned budget. Put a financial plan together that is as robust as you can, then work with your co-founders, advisors, and investors to check assumptions and ensure you've got everything.

Then, once you have completed this exercise, recognize that it will likely turn out to be wrong because things change. I generally plan 20% overhead on any major project for incidental things. This way, the pressure is alleviated from the plan having to be perfect because there is some slack in the budget to handle unexpected things. A diligent founder will review the events that dipped into the 20% overhead budget and update their model based on learning from the experience.

Be flexible

Unexpected projects come up. If you commit 100% of your team's capacity to the plan, then you have a tough decision to make when something inevitably arises. Either you have to jeopardize your plans because you need to allocate someone's time to the new side mission, taking away from the original plan, or you ignore the request because of lack of capacity.

This approach assumes that no issues arise that are important in light of the original plan. It's possible you planned correctly, but this may lead you to a solution that is not ideal due to doors that were inadvertently shut. Similar to the cash budgeting discussed earlier, when planning engineering work, leaving a buffer of 20% or so of capacity unallocated addresses this problem.

If you are using quarterly goals, break them down into weekly deliverables and leave a week per month for wiggle room for things to go wrong. As time goes on and you get better at forecasting accurately, you can dial down the amount of padding you are adding. If you are a first-time founder, or new with the team you are working with, 20% is a reasonable place to start.

We can never remove uncertainty from the equation, but with the proper tools in place we can manage it. These rules of thumb provide reasonable safeguards to complete projects on time and achieve their goals.

44

WORKING REMOTELY

In the winter of 2020, we were at a natural transition point in the company — we had recently closed our seed round in December 2019, and were starting to outgrow our office again. I had an offer letter out to a new employee who was joining us in late March. I didn't have any spare desk space for her, so I was planning to give her my desk and become nomadic myself. I was going to work from the sofa chair in the lobby on my laptop or something like that.

Sid and I looked into several office spaces in the same neighborhood. We had three proposals on our desk from different options for a three-year lease. I had a favorite I was gunning for. We had decided Sid would take responsibility for negotiating the lease and dealing with the logistics of moving our office while I kept focusing on developing the product.

One morning Sid called me into his office. "Hey this Covid thing looks pretty serious. Why don't we wait to see what happens before signing a three-year lease?"

Wise words. Two weeks later, California issued a shelterin-place order and banned most indoor gatherings of 10 people or more.

We held a companywide all-hands meeting to announce the transition, review logistics, and answer people's questions. Someone asked how long this was going to last. One employee set up a companywide poll before the all-hands meeting; the longest guess was three months. Most were two weeks or less.

I am an engineer, not an epidemiologist. But as a leader, you must have thoughtful answers to pressing events — geopolitical, macroeconomic, epidemiological, you name it. If a major news story affects your company, you need a narrative around how you are handling it.

"Well, the last time this happened in 1918, it took about two years to pass." I replied somewhat jokingly, afraid to make a precise prediction on something I knew so little about. It turned out to be just about bang on. Not bad for a non-answer.

Side note — I had just gotten the sales team a meter-wide gong with the Yembo logo on it. Like most bespoke purchases like this, I got it off Alibaba from a company based in Wuhan. At the time, the Chinese government ordered many factories to produce protective equipment like masks and gloves to make up for the shortfall in equipment as Covid surged. Just as the virus reached the US and supplies were stretched thin, the sales manager messaged me on WhatsApp and offered to sell me a case of 1,000 KN-95 masks and 70% isopropyl hand sanitizer. I accepted.

While most of San Diego was sold out, we were able to give every employee enough masks and sanitizer for themselves and their families and had a big bucket of free gear to give away outside our office.

When we still had hundreds of masks left after the office

closed, I donated to a friend who was a doctor at UC Irvine. It still blows my mind how my gong provider was able to be a more reliable source of masks to a legitimate medical facility than the local stores in those days.

As dramatic as those days were, the immediate transition to remote work was fairly smooth, at least at first. We already were used to asynchronous work with the India and Ukraine teams. The projects we were working on grew more complex than in our early days in the 200 sq. ft. office, so we'd have a small team brainstorm and design the product, then divide the implementation work into smaller tasks and work alongside the remote teams to build the features. There were problems around communication being harder, but those took some time to manifest themselves.

While we were shutting down the office and moving to work from home, I didn't have all the answers, so I diagnosed the problems and solicited ideas from the team.

- A lot of our work is interdependent. How do we stay on the same page while going remote?
- Can we remain as efficient as we are in the office when we go remote? What practices can we put into place to not lose what we have?
- How do we ensure people still have access to the information they need to do their job when they can't overhear things or have water cooler conversations?

About three months into Covid we felt we had a good system down. Here is what we learned:

Define core working hours.

When working from home, it can be tempting to stay in your pajamas until the afternoon, snack too much, and generally lose discipline over your day. To combat this, the engineering team agreed to generally work 9 a.m. to 5 p.m. unless exceptions arose. We'd update our Slack profile and Google Calendars with out-of-office notices if we'd ever not be working during core working hours. In addition, we'd do a daily standup meeting — cameras on — at 9:30 a.m. each morning. We'd use the slot to go over everything we planned on working on that day.

As the company grew, we stopped doing this because the workforce got used to remote work and didn't feel we needed the accountability to get out of bed anymore, and we also hired in different time zones, so 9:30 a.m. was the middle of the day for some folks on the east coast. Our core working hours have since shrunk to 10 a.m. to 2 p.m. Pacific to accommodate people in other time zones, and certain remote teams like the India team get exemptions due to the time difference. But having a core set of hours where the bulk of the workforce is reachable has turned out to be key.

No stigma around leaving meetings.

Back in the office, I could talk to one engineer and the whole engineering team would hear because we'd all be sitting in the same room. In remote work, if I set up a Zoom call with an engineer, no one else would hear it, so I'd have to repeat myself to get everyone on the same page.

To remedy this, I started sharing more in the morning standup meeting with the entire engineering team.

This had the obvious consequence of making the meeting too long.

What was happening was that people were sticking around because it's awkward to be the first person to hang up a call. So here we were in a productivity deadlock — with only two people talking about something but everyone else is sitting around, wanting to get back to work, but waiting for someone else to drop first before they will feel comfortable dropping. By making a company policy around dropping from meetings when you no longer feel you have anything to give or receive of value, we addressed this issue. We've found a quick courtesy is helpful (abruptly disappearing is weird) — "I don't think I have anything more to add to this topic so I'm going to drop out unless anyone else needs me for anything. Is that cool?"

Have an internal knowledge base.

We set up a knowledge base, dubbed Yembuddy, that covers not just how our product works, but also our workflows. It's a combination of written articles and explainer videos using screen recording software Loom. It replaced the patchwork of ad hoc conversations that were used for onboarding and training.

This way, a new employee can learn how our internal systems work, the interdependencies between teams, and general timing expectations. Setting this up at 10 employees took time, but the knowledge base still serves us today. It's much easier to share a link when someone has a simple question about how something works than to have the same conversation repeatedly.

One way to mitigate the overhead of writing and maintaining the knowledge base is simply to record a training call. Usually, there is some forcing function — an employee needs to know how to do something (perhaps, troubleshooting the continuous integration workflow). They ask someone who knows how it's set up, who in turn gets on a video chat to explain. By just recording that call, you can feed two birds with one loaf — answer the immediate question and answer for anyone else to follow who has a similar question.

45

INTERPERSONAL DYNAMICS CHANGE

The constant drive to achieve at a startup can be grueling, so it should not be surprising that people change as the environment changes. One of the more subtle-but-sinister pitfalls to look out for is the people around you changing.

In the early days, when the team is small, the product is fledgling, and ambitions are strong, there is an unspoken camaraderie that just naturally happens from being in the same place together. As the company grows and more layers of management come in, the founders will naturally not have as much time to spend with each employee as in the early days.

The dynamic has to change — a company of 30 cannot operate like a company of five. There are only so many hours in the day. This can be quite challenging for founders to impart as the company grows since often the culture in the early days just happened and wasn't an engineered outcome. As a result, when it comes time to intentionally impart the culture in a larger team, it can be difficult to implement.

And therein lies the pitfall — as a founder, you must push harder to get real feedback.

In our early days at Yembo, when the whole team was within arm's reach of each other, we got a certain amount of alignment for free due to proximity. Everyone knew what everyone else was working on. Everyone was working together toward the same goal.

Startups are generally execution-constrained, not idea constrained. We were no exception — we had lots of ideas, more than we could act on, and we routinely challenged each other to make sure we were working on the most pressing issues.

Brainstorming was a common part of the job. We'd share ideas freely and often the ideas were not very good. One of my early employees had prior experience working in translation (Rachel, who you met earlier). When our first customer asked to translate our entire product into German, I had some engineering-centric ideas on making translation easy that compromised the quality of the product and needed to be refined before it became viable.

It turns out just putting the translations in a spreadsheet strips the translator of valuable context, which can lead to elliptical word choices.

As the company grew, I noticed some newer employees were more cautious. They had reservations about telling a founder an idea wouldn't work. It took longer to find out when a project was behind schedule because no one wanted to float bad news up the reporting chain. The alignment we enjoyed in the early days no longer came for free.

I find it's best to be aware of this inevitable dynamic and mitigate it before it becomes a problem. To mitigate this, be willing to "go there first" when speaking candidly. In employer/employee relationships, the employee generally mirrors the demeanor of the employer.

If the employer is giving sugar-coated projections and glossing over major economic headwinds, why should it be expected for the employee to exhibit radical candor? Put another way, if you want a milquetoast outcome, act in a milquetoast way. For the communication to be effective, the leader needs to go first.

On the flip side, fostering a culture of openness and honesty signals to the team that these behaviors are expected, since leadership is holding themselves to the same standard.

Below are some phrases that I used to think leaders couldn't say, but today are second nature:

"I'm feeling nervous about this deadline."

I used to think a strong leader needed to portray confidence. And that's true; they do. But they are also not delusional, and if expectations seem too ambitious, it's ok to admit uncertainty about the plan. This opener invites scrutiny and collective problem-solving into the plan, which leads to the next line.

"I could use your help putting this plan together."

While it's true that leaders are ultimately responsible for plans, timelines, and budgets, a strong leader takes input from anyone who can bring valuable insight to the overall picture. Rather than presenting solutions to every problem, I now facilitate conversations with the right audience around problems we need to tackle. It's much easier to have buy-in on a plan when it is well thought out. Rather than holding an impossibly high bar for myself to come up with all the answers, I now solicit input and commit to a plan once everyone involved has had a chance to give their input.

"This next project is not going to be particularly fun."

Let's face it — sometimes grunt work comes up, and it just has to be done. One of our vendors had a security incident once and suggested we change every password for every system used to implement Yembo. It took five engineers two full days because we didn't have tooling in place to do things efficiently. Trying to sugarcoat everything and pretend it is valuable learning when you know full well it's not is dishonest. People are smart and know anyway. The only thing that suffers when you're dishonest is your credibility. So if I need someone to do something I know is particularly tedious or unglamorous, I generally tell them upfront that I recognize it's not the most exciting project. And I try to give them their pick after the project so they're not continually being dragged through the mud.

"What would you recommend focusing on next?"

Superhero management where the manager steps in to solve every problem works for a short time, but doesn't scale. The goal isn't to have a perfect plan off the bat in all cases. The goal is to have a reasonable plan by the time the main decisions need to be made. It's totally OK to ask people for their input on various aspects of the project in areas where they may have more insight than you.

One important caveat around being transparent about your feelings at work is in knowing the audience. It's generally better to praise somebody in public, and critique thoughtfully, with their best interests in mind, in private.

When the company wins, the team gets credit, and when things go wrong, only the people who need to know need to get involved in the specifics. Nobody likes being put on blast, and it's easy to steamroll over somebody in the name of radical candor.

Save yourself the fallout and critique in private.

46

WORKFLOWS HAVE A SHELF LIFE

Your processes and infrastructure all have a shelf life. It's helpful to remember that it's no one's fault when they break.

Like many software startups, we operate under the ethos at Yembo that it was our duty to ship fast.

Time-to-market is a valuable metric, and we wanted to get products into customers' hands as soon as possible so we could iterate with them and make things better. Startup 101.

This required a few months of building before the first version became viable, but we generally tried to get customer feedback as quickly as possible. Customers sometimes say one thing and do another. By monitoring actual adoption and usage, we were able to refine the product and deliver more value.

This policy manifested itself in the weekly release. Every Wednesday, the company released updates to the product. This was a tradition we started in our first year of operation and have proudly held onto as we have scaled.

On the surface, you can look at our release notes being

published every Wednesday and herald it as a hallmark of consistency. A commitment to an idealized goal.

The problem is, the work that went into keeping that cadence up is orders of magnitude more work than it was in the early days. One sign you need to retool is when everyone is doing their job, but the company isn't going where it needs to go.

When we first started, very few people would write code. This is a side effect of not having any employees yet. I'd generally write the API code myself, test it out, release it, then switch over to the frontend, write that code using the new APIs, test it out, then ship that. Everything I was shipping was code I wrote myself.

That is not sustainable if you're growing.

As the company grew, so did the complexity. We diverged into frontend and backend engineering teams, since the skillsets grew more specialized. Now each release was authored by multiple people. No one person had all the context in their head of how everything should work.

Anxiety grew around these Wednesday releases — Thursdays had disproportionately high volumes of bug tickets reported. We occasionally missed a Wednesday release window because we weren't confident in the code quality.

Part of me wondered if this was how things were destined to become. I had a friend who worked at a publicly traded enterprise software company, and they had two releases a year — one in June and one in December. Maybe the startup's growth trajectory was coupled with a gradual deceleration in release cycle until nirvana was achieved in semiannual releases.

I didn't know where the release cadence would end up, but I personally wanted to maintain the weekly release window. I polled the frontend engineers, the backend engineers, the customer success team that was graciously serving as the front line of defense for the Thursday morning firing squad of support tickets.

We started a Google Doc called "Releases Suck Because…" and encouraged people to add bullet points to the list. Apart from the catharsis this document provided, this approach had the benefit of centralizing all the problems that the forthcoming solution would need to resolve.

Below are the key findings we came up with:

- Too many authors are contributing code — no one person knows all the features going out in a release, and nobody feels they have time to understand each one.
- It is not clear what level of scrutiny code changes have gone through. The author may believe they will work, but unintended side effects crop up in production.
- It's hard to predict how code is going to fail, so we are dependent on customers reporting issues to learn of our defects.
- We don't have reliable monitoring systems in place. When something fails, we don't get alerted until a customer reports it to us.

Then we got to resolving the issues. Below are the solutions we put together:

- Build an internal knowledge base, Yembuddy, explaining the product features. Maintain it as part of the product release cycle — update the

Yembuddy articles when updating the corresponding product features.
- Define a list of scenarios that customers need to be able to do. Explain what is done and what the expected behavior should be. Run through this checklist on a candidate build before each release. Do not release with known defects.
- Require all code changes to be peer-reviewed before going live.
- Require the proposed code changes to have testing instructions, so the peer reviewer can know what to look out for.
- Require all code changes to be tested after passing peer review.

This approach cleaned up the process and restored weekly releases. Everything was great for about six months. Then a new crop of errors appeared:

- Yembuddy wasn't being updated reliably because it takes time to write good articles. The engineering team would have to decide between slowing down shipping features or skimping on documentation. They were picking to skimp on documentation.
- Features were sitting in review for days or weeks at a time. The extra steps slowed the process down.
- It grew harder to track the status of features while they were in progress since there were so many new steps between "To Do" and "Done."
- Engineers were prioritizing the tasks that were easier to finish, not necessarily the tasks that were most impactful to the company.

This led to a reprise "Releases Suck Because…" gripe doc, and a new round of updates:

- Have the QA team manage updating the Yembuddy documentation. They can provide an outline, screenshots, and main areas that need to be documented, because they already have that context while they are testing the feature. The engineering lead who is responsible for the feature just needs to review and edit versus write from scratch.
- Standardize the ticket statuses across our project management (Jira) and source code management (GitHub) systems. Automate the synchronization between the two so updating one drags along the status in the other.
- Automate tests where the process is repeatable. This alleviates the manual work required to test a proposed change to the codebase.
- Set timing expectations on each stage of the process so others know what to expect. For example, a peer is expected to review a pull request within one business day of being assigned. A QA tester is expected to test within one business day of the peer approving the code change.
- Use backlogged timing expectations as a signal when planning hiring — for example, the QA team consistently failing to meet the one-day service level agreement (SLA) is a signal that it's time to hire another QA tester.

This current approach has been in place for the last two

years, with only minor modifications needed as new parts of the product mature.

In hindsight, I should have planned on retooling our workflow every six months or so in the early days.

Because it's all a part of growing up. Fast.

47

WHERE AI IS HEADING

There is a mental model I have found to be useful, albeit a bit primitive, and that is to view workers in the tech economy as divided into two primary core competencies. First are the *innovators* who excel at rushing to the edge of what's possible, managing uncertainty, and willing the future into existence. But an economy full of innovators would be susceptible to perpetual distractions, and for that reason, the competency of *operators* are just as crucial. Operators are critical in scaling businesses, ensuring consistency and that systems are running well. Both sides work in tandem to achieve lasting economic growth.

Where we've been

Before charting the course ahead, it's helpful to review from where we've come. As the adage goes, history has a tendency to repeat itself, or at least rhyme.

Had I stayed employed at large tech companies, I would likely have developed into a formidable operator. A decade of steady employment at a large corporation is a major asset, especially for those with families. However, it's improbable that I would have had the diverse experiences that founding a startup has offered. I'd encourage others to consider their ambitions in the spectrum of innovators and operators — both are compelling in their own right and rewarding careers. In my experience, all too often individuals take opportunities as they come, without giving much thought to the trajectory they are setting themselves on.

An established company certainly wouldn't have required me to lunge to the restroom to call an engineer in India, or to learn the nuances of startup budgeting and raising capital, not to mention honing management skills across such a wide array of individuals with diverse backgrounds. In essence, the innovator path is akin to achieving an MBA in that you must master the skill of administering businesses, except if you do things right, it pays you instead of costing a fortune in tuition.

Here we are at the cusp of perhaps the largest industrial revolution ever, with the advent of AI reaching the mainstream. Like the industrial revolutions that came before it, there are profound heights to claim and precipitous depths to fall if society fails to get it right.

As consumers, governments, corporations, and individuals grapple with the implications of AI, we need input from everyone to make sure it speaks for all of us. Please do not sit idly and watch things play out — get involved and help the world figure out how to embed AI in the fabric of society.

Learn to use the latest tools. See where they work well and where they are lacking. In the gold rush era, it wasn't just the miners who made a fortune. The companies that sold picks and shovels did handsomely as well. One does not need to create AI to benefit from its effects on the economy.

I don't think I am hyperbolizing to say society is in the midst of being reinvented by AI. Will we achieve a utopia with universal basic income, where artificially intelligent agents willingly perform the mundane work of day-to-day life for us? Or will income inequity, already at points never before seen in the US economy, become further exaggerated? Perhaps AI will be regulated so severely its effects are marginalized at best, outlawed at worst? I'd encourage those considering this route to look to the United States' attempts on blanket bans in the Prohibition era for a lesson on how this approach may play out.

While no one can reliably predict the future precisely, and only a fool thinks they can, it seems fitting to make an attempt, towards the end of this book, on how one might spitball ideas for a startup AI company. While I am not going to venture into specific timing, there are a few trends I can see coming across the horizon.

AI tools become integrated into creative workflows

If AI democratizes the start of a lot of processes, but cannot finish until the technology matures more, what happens? Does it stall out, and the world determines the technology was overhyped?

I predict that the nascent AI technology will be welcomed in areas where people can handle incomplete work products. As long as generative AI makes mistakes that are obvious to a viewer, AI is not going to replace an artist. However, AI can have a place inside design tools. Need some creative inspiration or rough sketches of an idea? Imperfect outputs are acceptable at that stage of the process.

Need some ideas for an outline or some tagline ideas?

Document editing software can have brainstorming tools plugged in to make it easier to get over writer's block.

The role of governance becomes more prominent

Social media came of age in an era where data security and privacy was lightly regulated. After horror after horror became revealed, regulatory bodies eventually clued into what was happening and defined policies. Some pundits believe Europe's sweeping data privacy law GDPR, which came into effect in 2018, was largely in response to irresponsible internet companies at the time.

My hope is we learn from this mistake and get ahead of the curve in terms of governance this time around. Unfortunately, I have not seen much convincing work going on in this space on behalf of regulatory bodies. Startups that are creating cutting-edge AI technologies like OpenAI are filling in the gap by publishing their governing principles publicly so the public is at least aware of how decisions are made.

The AI Labels project (ailabels.org) provides badges that creators can use to self-certify the involvement of AI or its lack thereof in their work product. (Disclosure: I am the author of the AI Labels project, although I earn no financial compensation from my involvement).

Starting projects gets easier, but humans still make decisions

When technology revolutionizes a discipline, it dramatically reduces the cost of work in the area. Generally, the disruption makes an improvement that is an order of magnitude better, faster, or cheaper than its predecessor.

This has a democratizing effect where more people are able to participate in the area as a result of the increased accessibility. Before attempting to discern the future of AI, it is helpful to review how society got to this point.

In the early 1990s the main channels for communication were phone calls, mail, and fax machines. Then the Internet came along and suddenly the cost of sending a note to someone on the other side of the country was not the cost of a stamp, but essentially free. On top of that, messages could be interchanged immediately without the delay of the US Postal Service.

Before word processing tools, it would take weeks of manual typesetting to prepare a publication. Then computers democratized publishing, and now anyone can create a book.

The turn of the millennium saw the transition from Sony Walkman to iPods — 80 minutes of music in interchangeable discs to 1,000 songs in your pocket.

Moore's Law exponentially increased the power of computers affordable to laypeople, and as a result companies that published user-generated content became possible. YouTube's rise in the mid-2000s could not have happened without a similar revolution in the power of video editing tools driven by Moore's Law.

The smartphone revolution of the 2010s took the advancement of the semiconductor industry and made it so people could take the power of computing with them. New platforms such as ride hailing, meal delivery, and e-commerce were made possible thanks to the new underlying platform that laid the groundwork.

Think of a lake with an island in the middle, where the

level of the lake is rising. The areas that are closest to the shore are flooded first, and the highest elevations take the longest to be reached.

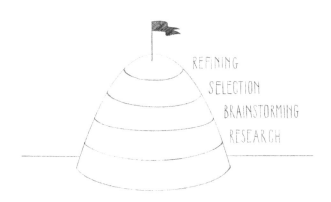

As technology decreases the barrier to entry to an industry, it is generally the most obvious use cases that get disrupted first. The simplest tasks, the most tedious, the ones that are the most clearly defined.

The self-driving car industry is a good example of this phenomenon. Self-driving cars work well in scenarios where the rules are clearly structured and behavior is predictable (e.g., highways), but they continue to struggle in complex city environments involving stop-and-go traffic, pedestrians, blocked lanes with parked vehicles, and complex right-of-way rules.

The AI revolution of the 2020s will follow similar fundamental trends. The cost of sifting through enormous datasets and extracting insights is becoming much less expensive, but this does not make everyone an analyst. We will likely see more businesses run by solopreneurs, but there will still be a human at the top for the foreseeable future.

As an exercise, look at AI-generated artwork from tools such as DALL-E 2, Midjourney, or Stable Diffusion. While it's remarkable how many ideas it can come up with in a relatively short amount of time, you generally don't have to look for very long before finding flaws.

And since AI is only loosely related to human biology, the flaws AI makes are not the same kind of flaws a human would make. I've seen portraits with three front teeth, animals with three hind legs, and hands with far too many fingers. These AI models are trained on vast troves of examples. They are emulating work products created by someone with the ability to reason, but they themselves do not have the ability to reason. This is why the mistakes are sometimes so obvious.

As illustrated by the self-driving car industry, the first 80% or so of an AI problem is relatively easy to solve, but improvements from there become exponentially more complicated. Algorithms can only asymptotically approach 100%, meaning perfection can never be truly attained.

What's next?

For people willing to look at it in a lateral manner, AI is providing a nearly infinite amount of opportunities. This is what happened with me. Moving and furniture as an AI business plan? Five years ago, it sounded extremely dubious. But here we are and it seems almost obvious.

Today, Yembo has delivered on this vision and added on another home service — the property insurance industry. We're building 3D computer vision technology to digitally reconstruct interiors of homes and streamline the underwriting and claims processes for insurance carriers. Our mission is to bring digital transformation to home service companies through best-in-class AI products. After insurance, there are many places we could go next.

I've talked a lot about brainstorming in this book. I would encourage everyone to brainstorm ideas for workflows that are not yet leveraging AI. The Internet came out, and a lot of people yawned. But the visionaries saw not what was, but what could be. And Internet ideas were developed that changed the world. I don't even need to list them because so many are household names.

That's exactly where we are with AI right now. Look carefully and deeply at the opportunity it affords to develop new ideas and businesses. And do it now, because AI is going to grow up fast.

48

THE BIG FINISH

During my journey in the startup world, I have learned one particular lesson that I believe to be more important than the others.

In this book we have:

covered lots of odd situations,

worked our way through several exercises,

and analyzed many expected and not-so-expected decisions made from my seven years of building an AI startup.

I believe it's important to plainly state the greater lesson so it stands out from the others.

The number one lesson I learned from my startup life is to have a wife like Lindsay.

ON RADIOHEAD
EPILOGUE

W hy is the title of this book *Grow Up Fast?* Starting a company, I found I needed to figure things out correctly and quickly. Many of these things I had never done before. Many of these things turned out not to be correct in hindsight. Mistakes are fantastic teachers.

In this book, you may have noticed a lot of references, oblique and overt, to the music of the band Radiohead. If I had to guess, probably 80% of the initial code I wrote for my company, Yembo, was created with Radiohead playing in the background.

You may be surprised. Why would someone do this? Venturing out to a world of uncertainty, perhaps something more upbeat would make more sense. To me, Radiohead's music is good for a lot of things. If you're a fan of Radiohead, you know what I mean. If you're not, let me try and explain it to you.

The music of Radiohead doesn't come right out and tell you what it is. You have to interpret it at almost a subliminal level. It makes your brain work. As successful as Justin Bieber is, no one ever accused his music of making your brain work. In fact, it may have the opposite effect.

I don't know if Radiohead intended their music to be environmental or ambient (Treefingers, anyone?). But for me, it is. I listen to it, and I work better.

Radiohead lyrics are notoriously asymmetric — the generic 4/4-time signature is often eschewed. Radiohead music makes you ask questions and think, which you are always doing when you are getting a startup going.

- What could go wrong?
- What new features do we need?
- What backgrounds are missing in our team?
- What signs should we see three or four months down the road that things are working?

Hundreds and hundreds of questions.

And I found that Radiohead's music helps me sort through those questions while I work.

Is it because much of the music of Radiohead is in the Dorian mode[1], which is, some say, a more reflective mode in music? Is it because much of the music of Radiohead seems unstructured, in irregular time signatures, and therefore doesn't get in the way of your thinking? That's beyond my pay grade.

What *is* within my pay grade is knowing when something makes me productive, when something helps me think better, and address problems more logically.

A big mug of black coffee does that. A speedy computer allows me to do that. Radiohead's music does that.

Lyrically, a lot of the music of Radiohead is about

problems. It's not happy music. It's music about things that can go wrong. You won't hear it at a club, I suspect. But you will hear it at work every day in my office, and I suspect in the offices of hundreds of thousands of people.

Radiohead's music has been a constant touchstone in my work and life. If you've never listened to their music, go to your favorite streaming service, pick a Radiohead playlist, turn the volume down low, and start doing some work. More likely than not, you'll be a fan after two hours.

Even if not, you will have gotten a lot done.

READING LIST

Throughout my time building Yembo, I have found several books to be illuminating. I've shared the list below, and it's worth mentioning I'm simply a satisfied reader. I have no financial interest in promoting any of the following books:

Building Startups

- *Zero to One: Notes on Startups, or How to Build the Future* by Peter Thiel and Blake Masters
- *The Hard Thing About Hard Things: Building a Business When There Are No Easy Answers* by Ben Horowitz
- *The Lean Startup: How Today's Entrepreneurs Use Continuous Innovation to Create Radically Successful Businesses* by Eric Ries
- *Value Proposition Design: How to Create Products and Services Customers Want* by Alexander Osterwalder, Yves Pigneur, Gregory Bernarda, and Alan Smith

- *Crossing the Chasm: Marketing and Selling Disruptive Products to Mainstream Customers* by Geoffrey A. Moore
- *Nail It then Scale It: The Entrepreneur's Guide to Creating and Managing Breakthrough Innovation* by Nathan R. Furr

Making Great Presentations

- *slide:ology: The Art and Science of Creating Great Presentations* by Nancy Duarte

Understanding Venture Capitalism

- *Venture Deals: Be Smarter Than Your Lawyer and Venture Capitalist* by Brad Feld and Jason Mendelson

Product Management and Design

- *Lean Customer Development: Building Products Your Customers Will Buy* by Cindy Alvarez
- *Hooked: How to Build Habit-Forming Products* by Eyal Nir
- *The Design Of Everyday Things* by Don Norman
- *Build: An Unorthodox Guide to Making Things Worth Making* by Tony Fadell
- *Laying The Foundations: How to Design Websites and Products Systematically* by Andrew Couldwell
- *Escaping the Build Trap: How Effective Product Management Creates Real Value* by Melissa Perri

Running the Company

- *The Great CEO Within: The Tactical Guide to Company Building* by Matt Mochary
- *The Challenger Sale: Taking Control of the Customer Conversation* by Matthew Dixon and Brent Adamson

ENDNOTES

1. The Future on Line One

1. Stapleton, Richard J., and Gene Murkison. 1990. "Scripts and Entrepreneurship." *Transactional Analysis Journal* 20 (3): 193—97. https://doi.org/10.1177/036215379002000309.
2. "Steve Altman, Qualcomm Vice Chairman, to Retire." n.d. Qualcomm.com. Accessed April 30, 2023. https://www.qualcomm.com/news/releases/2013/10/steve-altman-qualcomm-vice-chairman-retire.

2. Putting in The Work

1. Weir, Andy. 2014. *The Martian*. Broadway Books.
2. Godefroy, Alexandre F. n.d. Hair-Dressing Device. 389803. *US Patent*, filed April 13, 1888.
3. Holyfield, Evander. n.d. https://www.youtube.com/watch?v=rAmnGJINErY&t=117s.
4. Wreglesworth, Rob. 2020. "Does More Power Mean Better Sound?" *Musician's HQ* (blog). July 14, 2020. https://musicianshq.com/does-more-power-mean-better-sound/.
5. Christensen, Clayton M., Taddy Hall, Karen Dillon, and David S. Duncan. 2016. "Know Your Customers' 'Jobs to Be Done.'" *Harvard Business Review*, September 1, 2016. https://hbr.org/2016/09/know-your-customers-jobs-to-be-done.

3. Speak the Language

1. Goldman, Ryan, Jonathan Friedman, and Zachary Rattner. 2018. System and method for an enhanced hair dryer. 10,405,630. *Patent*, filed July 29, 2017, and issued February 1, 2018.

4. A Five-Year Project

1. "AirPods Pro." n.d. Apple. Accessed April 30, 2023. https://www.apple.com/airpods-pro/.

5. Moving On

1. N.d. Researchgate.net. Accessed April 30, 2023. https://www.researchgate.net/publication/259369472_Analysing_Nascent_Entrepreneurs'_Behaviour_through_Intention-Based_Models.

6. Machine Vision

1. Hempel, Jessi. 2018. "Fei-Fei Li's Quest to Make AI Better for Humanity." *Wired*, November 13, 2018. https://www.wired.com/story/fei-fei-li-artificial-intelligence-humanity/.

2. Miller, George A. 1993. "WordNet: A Lexical Database for English." In *Proceedings of the Workshop on Human Language Technology — HLT '93.* Morristown, NJ, USA: Association for Computational Linguistics.

3. "Wordnets in the World." n.d. Globalwordnet.org. Accessed April 30, 2023. http://globalwordnet.org/resources/wordnets-in-the-world/.

4. "ImageNet." n.d. Image-net.org. Accessed April 30, 2023. https://www.image-net.org/challenges/LSVRC/.

5. labeling interface. n.d. "What I Learned from Competing against a ConvNet on ImageNet." GitHub.Io. Accessed April 30, 2023. http://karpathy.GitHub.io/2014/09/02/what-i-learned-from-competing-against-a-convnet-on-imagenet/.

6. "Time for AI to Cross the Human Performance Range in ImageNet Image Classification." 2020. AI Impacts. October 19, 2020. https://aiimpacts.org/time-for-ai-to-cross-the-human-performance-range-in-imagenet-image-classification/.

7. Krizhevsky, Alex, Ilya Sutskever, and Geoffrey E. Hinton. 2017. "ImageNet Classification with Deep Convolutional Neural Networks." *Communications of the ACM* 60 (6): 84—90. https://doi.org/10.1145/3065386.

8. "ImageNet Large Scale Visual Recognition Competition 2012 (ILSVRC2012)." n.d. Image-net.org. Accessed April 30, 2023. https://image-net.org/challenges/LSVRC/2012/results.html.

9. "NVIDIA GeForce RTX 3090 & 3090 Ti Graphics Cards." n.d. NVIDIA. Accessed April 30, 2023. https://www.nvidia.com/en-us/geforce/graphics-cards/30-series/rtx-3090-3090ti/; "Is the Human

Brain a Biological Computer?" n.d. Princeton.edu. Accessed April 30, 2023. https://press.princeton.edu/ideas/is-the-human-brain-a-biological-computer.

10. "ImageNet Winning CNN Architectures (ILSVRC)." n.d. Kaggle.com. Accessed April 30, 2023. https://www.kaggle.com/getting-started/149448.

11. Linn, Allison. 2015. "Microsoft Researchers Win ImageNet Computer Vision Challenge." The AI Blog. December 10, 2015. https://blogs.microsoft.com/ai/microsoft-researchers-win-imagenet-computer-vision-challenge/.

12. He, Kaiming, Xiangyu Zhang, Shaoqing Ren, and Jian Sun. 2015. "Deep Residual Learning for Image Recognition." *ArXiv [Cs.CV]*. http://arxiv.org/abs/1512.03385.

12. Naming is Hard

1. "Yembo, Ethiopia — Geographical Names, Map, Geographic Coordinates." n.d. Geographic.org. Accessed April 30, 2023. https://geographic.org/geographic_names/name.php?uni=-879487&fid=1721&c=ethiopia.

2. *The IT Crowd — Series 3 Episode 5*. n.d. Accessed June 2, 2023. https://www.channel4.com/programmes/the-it-crowd/on-demand/45363-005.

3. Saul, Derek. 2021. "Facebook Owner Pays $60 Million for 'Meta' Name Rights." Forbes. December 13, 2021. https://www.forbes.com/sites/dereksaul/2021/12/13/facebook-owner-pays-60-million-for-meta-name-rights.

13. Decision Time

1. Dylan, Bob. 1979. *Gotta Serve Somebody*. Columbia.

17. The Time Warp

1. "GarageBand for Mac." n.d. Apple. Accessed April 30, 2023. https://www.apple.com/mac/garageband/.

2. "The Beatles and Multitrack Recording." n.d. National Museums Liverpool. Accessed April 30, 2023. https://www.liverpoolmuseums.org.uk/beatles-and-multitrack-recording.

21. The Dangers of Feedback

1. Ries, Eric. 2012. *The Lean Startup: How Today's Entrepreneurs Use Continuous Innovation to Create Radically Successful Businesses*. Nikken BP Sha.
2. "Explainers." n.d. Tag.w3.org. Accessed June 2, 2023. https://tag.w3.org/explainers/.

22. Low Pass Filter

1. Eno, Brian. 2021 Interview by Rick Rubin. https://youtu.be/BOtrCYyf4cg?t=1408.

25. Finding a Co-Founder

1. Carson, Biz. 2021. "How Many Founders Does a Startup Really Need?" Protocol. July 10, 2021. https://www.protocol.com/newsletters/pipeline/how-to-find-a-co-founder.

28. As Small as Possible

1. *The New York Times*. 1989. "Hollywood's Most Secret Agent," July 9, 1989. https://www.nytimes.com/1989/07/09/magazine/hollywood-s-most-secret-agent.html.
2. N.d. Inc.com. Accessed April 30, 2023. https://www.inc.com/nicholas-sonnenberg/jeff-bezos-2-pizza-rule-meetings-at-amazon.html.

30. Celebrating Wins

1. N.d. Congress.gov. Accessed April 30, 2023. https://constitution.congress.gov/browse/essay/artI-S8-C8-4-1/ALDE_00013066/.

32. Startup Folk: Tiana in Her Own Words

1. Meiling, Brittany. 2018. "Moving Sucks. Ex-Qualcomm Engineers Build AI Startup Yembo to Help." *San Diego Union-Tribune*, November 3, 2018. https://www.sandiegouniontribune.com/business/technology/sd-fi-yembo-moving-app-20181103-story.html.

34. Micromanagement: Get off my Case

1. Steigrad, Alexandra, and Nicolas Vega. 2019. "Apple's Hollywood Venture Marred by 'Intrusive' Execs, Including Tim Cook." *New York Post*, March 3, 2019. https://nypost.com/2019/03/03/appless-hollywood-venture-marred-by-intrusive-execs/.

35. Using Deadlines Effectively

1. Altman, Sam. 2021. "Move Faster. Slowness Anywhere Justifies Slowness Everywhere.2021 Instead of 2022. This Week Instead of next Week. Today Instead of Tomorrow.Moving Fast Compounds so Much More than People Realize." Twitter. January 1, 2021. https://twitter.com/sama/status/1345140364995227648?lang=en.
2. N.d. Carta.com. Accessed June 3, 2023. https://carta.com/blog/venture-fundraising-early-stage-startups-2022/

36. Should I Stay?

1. N.d. Carta.com. Accessed April 30, 2023. https://carta.com/blog/employment-tenure-startups/.

39. On The Payroll

1. Hansberry, Lorraine. 1994. *Raisin in the Sun*. New York, NY: Vintage Books.

40. Letting Go to Let Others Flourish

1. N.d. Twilio.com. Accessed April 30, 2023. https://customers.twilio.com/2438/yembo/.

On Radiohead

1. Malawey, Victoria. 2012. "Ear Training with the Music of Radiohead." *Indiana Theory Review* 30 (2): 27—64. http://www.jstor.org/stable/24045402.

GLOSSARY

- **Accelerometer**: A sensor that detects the movements and changes in motion of an object. Accelerometers are used in smartphones to detect motion.
- **Algorithm**: A set of instructions that a computer program follows to solve a problem or complete a task. Algorithms are used to automate processes to make them operate faster and more efficiently.
- **Alibaba**: A China-based e-commerce company founded by Jack Ma in 1999. Unlike most US-based e-commerce companies, Alibaba facilitates communication directly between purchasers and factories, affording a great degree of flexibility in the products being purchased.
- **Ambient**: In music theory, ambient refers to music that is used to set a specific mood or tone, or act as a quiet auditory environment.

- **Application Programming Interface (API)**: A way for computer programs or source code to communicate with each other.
- **Asymmetric**: Not balanced or symmetrical. This can be in reference to the appearance of an object, or in describing power or influence, when one side has more sway than the other.
- **Asymptotically**: In mathematics, an asymptotic function approaches a limit but never reaches that limit. For example, the function $y = 1/x$ asymptotically approaches zero, but there is no value for x that makes $y = 0$.
- **Asynchronous**: Not happening at the same time or in conjunction with something else. For example, communicating via email is asynchronous, since the recipient can read and reply on their own time as opposed to having to respond immediately.
- **Chief Financial Officer (CFO)**: An executive role responsible for managing the company's finances.
- **Codebase**: The collection of source code files that make up a computer program. The codebase can be large and complex, especially for bigger software applications like operating systems.
- **Consumables**: Items that are used up during a process and need to be replaced regularly to ensure continued function of the process. An example of a consumable would be printer ink cartridges and paper, as a printer needs these to function properly and these items are used up during normal operation of the device.

- **Convolutional**: A mathematical operation that can be used to process images and extract useful features or patterns from an image.
- **Convolutional Neural Networks (CNNs / ConvNets)**: A specific type of deep learning algorithm that enables differentiation between images using the convolutional mathematical operation. CNNs are commonly used in object recognition tasks.
- **CrashLoopBackOff**: An error message that can occur when running a software application with Kubernetes. When an application crashes, Kubernetes automatically tries to restart it. If the application keeps crashing despite Kubernetes's attempts to restart it, Kubernetes will stop trying to restart it. When this scenario occurs, the application's status becomes **CrashLoopBackOff**.
- **Customer Relationship Manager (CRM)**: Software used for managing a company's relationships with prospects and clients.
- **Epidemiological**: The study of how diseases spread and affect populations for the purpose of preventing and controlling disease outbreaks. This can involve tracking the spread of disease and analyzing risk factors and other data to identify patterns.
- **GarageBand**: Music creation software developed by Apple allowing for recording, mixing, and editing music. It allows users to create and record music on Apple devices, and comes with a variety of built-in instruments and sound effects.

- **General Data Protection Regulation (GDPR)**: A robust and sweeping data privacy law protecting personal data for residents of the European Union. The law gives protected individuals substantial control over who can access their data and what kinds of processing can be done to the data.
- **GitHub**: A web-based platform owned by Microsoft that developers use to share their code. The platform allows other developers to view code and make changes. Developers can suggest improvements to other developer's code, which is a valuable tool for collaboration among software developers.
- **Grade Point Average (GPA)**: A numerical score that indicates academic performance.
- **Halogen**: A group of elements on the periodic table consisting of fluorine, chlorine, bromine, iodine, astatine, and tennessine. Quartz tungsten halogen lamps can be used to emit visible light, or heat if tuned to emit primarily in the infrared spectrum.
- **Human Resources (HR)**: The division of a business responsible for recruiting, managing, and training personnel.
- **ImageNet**: A dataset that contains millions of images which have been labeled with the object it contains. The images are divided into different categories such as "animals" and "vehicles", and also includes a set of challenge categories which are more complex and require more advanced object recognition algorithms. ImageNet is used to

train algorithms and is widely used in machine learning.

- **Interdependencies**: The relationship between two or more things that rely on each other for their functioning for success. This can be on a small scale, such as a business needing supplies and the supplier needing revenue from the business, or on a larger scale, such as two countries' economies being dependent on each other.
- **Internal Revenue Service (IRS)**: The US government agency responsible for collecting US federal taxes.
- **Jira**: Project management and bug tracking software developed by Atlassian.
- **Kubernetes (k8s)**: An open source project initially created by Google used to deploy and manage cloud infrastructure. It can automatically deploy, manage, and scale applications, which allows developers to focus on building applications rather than managing infrastructure.
- **Letter of Intent (LOI)**: A legal document that outlines an agreement between two or more parties. While there are variations, LOIs are generally non-binding, meaning either party can terminate at any time. LOIs typically outline the terms of a proposed project between two parties, which could include items such as the responsibilities of each party, financial agreements, and legal considerations. Letters of Intent are often used as a preliminary step before drafting a more formal agreement.

- **Lexical**: The vocabulary or set of words used in a field of study. An example of this would be the lexical field of computer science containing words such as "algorithm", "database", and "code". The understanding of the lexical field of a particular subject can help you to better understand the concepts and ideas used in the particular field of study.
- **Magnetic Resonance Imaging (MRI)**: Non-invasive technology that provides detailed three-dimensional imaging inside a body.
- **Master of Business Administration (MBA)**: A postgraduate degree focused on administering and operating businesses.
- **Minimum Viable Product**: A development strategy used in product creation where a new product is developed with just enough features to satisfy early adopters. The primary purpose of an MVP is to test the product hypothesis with minimal resources and gather user feedback for future development.
- **Moore's Law**: An observation made by Gordon Moore, co-founder of Intel, that the number of transistors in a chip doubles approximately every two years. This trajectory has made progressive enhancements in the field of computing possible since the 1970s.
- **National Collegiate Athletic Association (NCAA)**: A nonprofit organization that manages and governs student athletics.
- **Nichrome**: An alloy made from nickel, chromium, and other metals like iron or titanium.

It is primarily used for its high resistance and its ability to avoid corrosion. Nichrome is able to get very hot without melting or losing its shape, which makes it useful for items such as heating elements and resistance wires.

- **Non-Disclosure Agreement (NDA)**: A legal contract that prohibits one or more parties from sharing confidential information with others. This type of agreement is commonly used by businesses to prevent their competitors or the public from learning about their operations. The agreement specifies what information is considered confidential, who is bound by the agreement, and the consequences if the agreement were to be breached.
- **Patent Troll**: A pejorative term describing an individual or company that ships no products of their own, hoards patents, and attempts to generate revenue by accusing other entities of infringing their patents.
- **Quartz**: A mineral known for its hardness, durability, and unique crystal structure. Quartz is used in electronic devices as a timekeeper since it can create electrical signals that are highly precise. Quartz tungsten halogen lamps can be used to emit visible light, or heat if tuned to emit in the infrared spectrum.
- **Scope Creep:** Scope creep refers to the uncontrolled expansion of a project's goals, objectives, or features beyond its original agreed-upon scope. This often happens due to changes or additions made after the project has already

started, without corresponding increases in resources, time, or budget. If not properly managed, scope creep can lead to project delays, cost overruns, and failure to meet the initial objectives.

- **Semantically**: The relationship between words or symbols and their meanings.
- **Service Level Agreement (SLA)**: A set of expectations, often memorialized in a legal document, that describes the products and services to be delivered from a vendor to a client. For example, a software product may guarantee 99.99% uptime throughout the month in the SLA, with financial penalties if the terms are not met.
- **Solopreneurs**: A combination of the terms "solo" and "entrepreneur". Individuals who start and operate a business on their own.
- **Synchronous**: Happening at the same time or in coordination with another event. For example, two people having a face-to-face conversation is an example of synchronous communication, since both parties must be involved at the same time.
- **Synset**: A combination of the terms "synonym" and "set". A group of words that are closely related in meaning and can mostly be used interchangeably. Synsets are commonly used in computational linguistics and machine learning to help computers understand the meanings of words and their relationships to other words.
- **Tungsten**: A rare metal that is known for its strength and high melting point. It is commonly used in the filament of incandescent light bulbs.

Quartz tungsten halogen lamps can be used to emit visible light, or heat if tuned to emit in the infrared spectrum.

- **Underwriters Laboratories (UL)**: A company founded in 1894 that tests and certifies products for safety and sustainability. Their certifications are commonly required in various industries, such as healthcare, construction, and energy. When products are tested by Underwriters Laboratories, they are checked to make sure they meet certain safety standards, such as fire or shock resistance.
- **Value Proposition**: The benefits a company provides to its customers. For example, a grocery store's value proposition may be quality produce at affordable prices.
- **Venture Capital**: A form of private equity investing typically geared toward early-stage startups, often in the technology industry.
- **Wattage**: A unit of measurement used to express the rate of energy consumption or transfer over time. Understanding the wattage of a device can help one determine how much it will cost to run, or how long the device will run when powered off of a battery.
- **WordNet**: A database for English words that organizes words and concepts into synsets. WordNet is widely used in machine learning and computational linguistics. This helps computers learn the relationships between words and concepts, which helps improve tasks like text analysis and language translation.

- **World Wide Web Consortium (W3C)**: An international community that defines the standards for the web. It was founded in 1994 by Tim Berners-Lee, one of the creators of the first web browser.
- **Wunderkind**: A German term that describes a young person who is exceptionally talented in a particular field, a "prodigy". This can relate to various fields such as sports, music, or academics.
- **Yembuddy**: Yembo's internal knowledge base containing documentation and how-to guides for various product features.

FROM OUR FRIENDS AT VOLO BEAUTY

Go cordless with VOLO Beauty.
Use coupon code **GROWUPFAST** for 15% off.
https://volobeauty.com/discount/GROWUPFAST